5A

FOCUS
ON
GRAMMAR

AN INTEGRATED SKILLS APPROACH

THIRD EDITION

RACHEL SPACK KOCH
WITH KEITH S. FOLSE

PEARSON
Longman

FOCUS ON GRAMMAR 5A: An Integrated Skills Approach
Workbook

Pearson Education, 10 Bank Street, White Plains, NY 10606

Staff credits: The people who made up the *Focus on Grammar 5 Workbook* team, representing
editorial, production, design, and manufacturing, are: Rhea Banker, Aerin Csigay, Christine
Edmonds, Nancy Flaggman, Ann France, Diana George, Laura Le Dréan, and Mykan White.
Cover images: Large shell, Nick Koudis, RF; background, Comstock Images, RF
Text design: Quorum Creative Services, Rhea Banker
Text composition: ElectraGraphics, Inc.
Text font: 11/13 Sabon, 10/13 Myriad Roman

Illustrator: Steven Schulman, pp. 116, 117.
Text credits: **p. 8** Table from the Population Reference Bureau, http://www.prb.org. Used with per-
mission. **p. 15** Based on an article from *The New York Times*, July 26, 1998, by Lois Smith Brady.
Names and dates have been changed. **p. 26** Graph based on United Nations *World Urbanization
Prospects*, 2003 revision. **p. 50** Adapted from *The Cambridge Encyclopedia of Language*, by David
Crystal. Cambridge University Press, 1987. **p. 54** Menu from the Mitsitam Native Foods Café,
National Museum of the American Indian, Washington, D.C. Used with permission. **p. 70** Based
on the article *Is English Changing?*, from the website of the Linguistic Society of America,
www.lsadc.org. **p. 82** Based on an article from *The Wall Street Journal*, July 29, 1994, by Eric
Morgenthaler. **p. 107** Based on *The Discovery of Radium, Address by Madame M. Curie at Vassar
College, May 14, 1921*, Ellen S. Richards Monographs No. 2 (Poughkeepsie: Vassar College, 1921).
pp. 112, 180 Based on material from *Amazing Facts*, by Richard B. Manchester. New York: Bristol
Park Books, 1991. **p. 123** Based on an article in *The Washington Post*, October 27, 2004, by
Anthony Faiola; an article in *The Mainichi Daily News*, March 6, 2003, by Makoto Kawanabe and
Mainichi Shimbun; and an article on EverestNews.com, March 1, 2004. **p. 148** Based on an online
article from *The Washington Post*, January 8, 2005, by Don Oldenburg; and an online article from
National Geographic News, January 4, 2005, by Maryann Mott. **p. 189** Based on material from
Extraordinary Origins of Everyday Things, by Charles Panati. Perennial Library, Harper & Row,
1987, revised 1989.
Photo credits: **p. 21** Robert Koene/Getty Images; **p. 24** *(left)* Manoj Shah/Getty Images, *(right)* Image
Source Limited/Index Stock Imagery; **p. 155** Manuel Zambrana/Corbis.

ISBN: 0-13-191283-6 (Workbook A)

LONGMAN ON THE **WEB**

Longman.com offers online resources for
teachers and students. Access our Companion
Websites, our online catalog, and our local
offices around the world.

Visit us at **longman.com**.

Printed in the United States of America
1 2 3 4 5 6 7 8 9 10—ML—12 11 10 09 08 07 06 05

Contents

About the Authors

Rachel Spack Koch has been developing ESL materials and has taught ESL for many years, principally at the University of Miami, and also at Harvard University, Bellevue Community College, and Miami-Dade College. In addition to the *Focus on Grammar 5 Workbook,* she has contributed to other widely used ESL workbooks. A participant in and developer of interactive student activities on the Internet since the early 1990s, she also designs and writes content for ESL software.

Keith S. Folse has taught English for more than twenty-five years in many places, including the United States, Saudi Arabia, Kuwait, Malaysia, and Japan. He has a Ph.D. in Second Language Acquisition and Instructional Technology. He has written numerous other ESL books on grammar, composition, reading, speaking, and TOEFL. He regularly does workshops and presentations for teachers all over the world.

Present and Future Time

1 | USING VERB FORMS

A new play is opening tonight. The curtain rises and we see Paul, a new father, talking and singing to his three-week-old daughter. Complete the passage. Circle the correct verb forms.

Oh, little daughter! You are the best thing that <u>is coming /</u> (has come) into our lives.
                                                                                                1.

We <u>are going to have / have had</u> so many wonderful years together. Soon
              2.

you <u>'ll be walking / 're walking</u>. Then you <u>'ll go / 've gone</u> to school, and you <u>will have / have</u> friends.
          3.   4.   5.

The next thing you know, I <u>will be walking / have been walking</u> down the aisle with you
                                              6.

at your wedding.

Oh, little one! Time flies! Too soon you <u>will have grown / will have been growing</u> up and
                                                          7.

<u>will have had / will have</u> a life of your own, with children of your own. I <u>am / will be</u> a
          8.   9.

grandfather. But I <u>am thinking / think</u> about your life too far into the future. We <u>have / are having</u>
                              10.   11.

a lot of years between now and then.

He hums and sings:

Hush, little baby, don't say a word, Papa <u>'s going to buy / buys</u> you a mockingbird.
                                                          12.

And if that mockingbird <u>doesn't sing / isn't singing</u>, Papa <u>'s going to buy / 's buying</u> you a
                                      13.   14.

diamond ring.

Shh! Shh! Why <u>do you cry / are you crying</u>? Everything's going to be all right.
                          15.

2 | DISTINGUISHING ACTIONS IN THE PRESENT AND FUTURE TIME

*Read this letter from Goodman and Greene, a financial planning firm. In each set of two sentences, write **1** in front of the action that happens first, and **2** in front of the action that happens second.*

Dear Professional: G&G

As you read this, retirement seems very far away.

1. You have a good income, and you're getting a nice raise in January.

   _1_   You have a good income.

   _2_   You get a nice raise in January.

2. If you save a little more this year, you'll be able to buy a new home soon.

   _____   You save a little more.

   _____   You are able to buy a new home.

3. You can take a long vacation as soon as you have the time.

   _____   You can take a long vacation.

   _____   You have the time.

4. By the time your children are ready for college, you will have saved enough money for their tuition.

   _____   Your children are ready for college.

   _____   You have the money you need for their tuition.

5. When you retire, you will have been working steadily for 35 years.

   _____   You retire.

   _____   You work steadily.

6. You will have earned the comfortable life that you are dreaming about.

   _____   You earn the comfortable life.

   _____   You dream about the comfortable life.

7. However, you need to plan carefully long before you retire.

   _____   You retire.

   _____   You plan carefully.

Call our office today for an appointment with one of our experienced financial planners. He or she will discuss your unique situation with you and suggest which mix of stocks, bonds, and other financial instruments are best for you.

8. After you have met with him or her, you will feel confident about your financial future.

   _____   You meet with him or her.

   _____   You feel confident.

Sincerely yours,

Boris M. Goodman

Boris M. Goodman, President

3 | DISTINGUISHING ACTIONS IN THE PRESENT AND FUTURE TIME

*Read the text of an e-mail from Lucia to her close friend Thelma. Over each underlined phrase, indicate whether the time refers to the **Present** (P) or **Future** (F). Add a check mark (✓) if the time includes reference to the past.*

Hi, Thelma:

      ^P <u>I'm updating</u> my resume right now. ^F <u>I'm sending</u> it out as soon as possible—along with a cover letter—to about fifty advertising firms.

      A draft of the cover letter is attached. <u>I don't think</u> it has enough pizzazz, so <u>I'm sending</u> it to you right now in the hopes that <u>you will improve</u> it. As you can see, <u>I haven't finished it</u>—I am really stuck. <u>I've written</u> two previous drafts of this letter, and I am still not satisfied with it.

      <u>I'm thinking</u> about posting my resume on one of those job sites on the Internet. What <u>do you think</u> about that? Of course, <u>I'll also send</u> the resume, along with the cover letter, to the firms that I am interested in. Is it OK <u>if I send</u> my resume and cover letter by e-mail, or will the Human Resources people pay more attention <u>if they receive</u> hard copies in the mail?

      <u>If I post</u> my resume on the job site tonight and send e-mails to fifty companies, <u>I'll get</u> some response by the end of the week, don't you think? In fact, by this time next week, <u>I probably will have heard</u> from ten or fifteen different firms.

      I'll redo the resume and the letter with your suggestions as soon as <u>I hear</u> from you. <u>I'll be sitting</u> here at my computer <u>waiting</u> for your reply! Thanks in advance for your help. <u>I'm counting</u> on you, as I have done for all these years that we have been friends.

—Lucia

4 | USING VERB FORMS

Read this letter from a tour director, sent just prior to a group's departure for Antarctica.
Complete the letter by writing the correct forms of the verbs in parentheses.

Destination: Antarctica

Dear Traveler:

Enclosed are your tickets, your itinerary, your luggage tags, and the passenger list for

your trip to Argentina and Antarctica on the 30th of this month. We know that this is

going to be the trip of your life!

We will meet in the GlobeAir lounge in Miami when everybody _____*arrives*_____
1. (arrive)

from other flights. After we _____ each other at a small "Welcome Aboard"
2. (greet)

party, we'll depart for Buenos Aires. As soon as you _____ the ship, you
3. (board)

_____ the adventure in the air!
4. (feel)

After a one-day stopover in Buenos Aires, we'll continue on to Antarctica. As you

_____ into the world's most unspoiled continent, you'll see penguins,
5. (venture)

glaciers, and spectacular scenery. You'll marvel at the clear, cold air and the stunning,

high mountains. Our experienced naturalists will describe the area before you actually

_____ the bays by small landing craft.
6. (explore)

After we _____ at sea for two weeks, you _____ to return to
7. (be)   **8. (want / not)**

your normal routine. You _____ unique sights and adventures for the past
9. (experience)

two weeks. By the time you _____ to Buenos Aires on the 15th, you
10. (return)

_____ the ultimate in adventure cruising.
11. (experience)

I look forward to meeting you all and to our exciting trip together!

Truly yours,

Margaret de Bono

Margaret de Bono, Tour Director

5 | USING VERB FORMS IN SENTENCES WITH FUTURE TIME CLAUSES

At Beautiville Central High School, elections were held for the following distinctions and won by the following graduates. These results were listed in the BCHS yearbook. Read the predictions about these graduates. Complete the predictions by writing the correct forms of the verbs in parentheses.

TITLE	WINNER
Most Likely to Succeed	Al Albert
Funniest	Bob Bradley
Most Athletic	Fred Fenson
Best Dressed	Gail George
Most Popular	Harry Hernández
Best Natured	Jenny James
Cleverest	Katherine Klumper
Class Sweethearts	Rose Rincón and Bob Bradley

HERE'S WHAT WE CAN EXPECT FROM OUR GRADUATING SENIORS IN THE NEXT DECADE

Several of our classmates are sure to make it big. Al Albert has always had a passion for the

law and great skill in debating. There is no doubt that Al will be a fine lawyer, and perhaps he

____*will become*____ a governor or a senator one day. Our class comedian, Bob Bradley, will
    1. (become)

certainly be a very successful stand-up comic. When they _____ the prizes for the best
                                2. (award)

television comedy star in 10 years, Bob is going to win one, for sure. And what about our star

athlete, Fred Fenson? Fred has won a football scholarship to State University. We think that he

will be a star there and that before he _____ from State, he will have received several
                       3. (graduate)

lucrative offers from professional football teams. Next, it should come as no surprise that the

best-dressed person in our graduating class, Gail George, has accepted a job at *Glamourama*

Magazine; we fully expect that by the time five years go by, everyone in the fashion world

_____ her name. Harry Hernández will have tons of friends, wherever life leads him.
  4. (hear)

As the most popular person in our class, Harry _____ in any career he undertakes.
                                 5. (succeed)

Jenny James, with her warm and caring personality, is going to become a fine social worker. This year, though, she _____ some time off to work in a new program with
6. (take)

underprivileged children. The program _____ for just two weeks when Jenny starts
7. (operate)

next month. A year after that, Jenny will enter City College of Social Work. And our clever

Katherine Klumper? She _____ president of a big company, we predict. About to enter
8. (become)

Cornell University as a sophomore, she _____ both her B.A. and M.B.A. within four
9. (get)

years. There are two people we feel especially fond of: Rose Rincón and Bob Bradley, our class

sweethearts. They _____ together for the past five years; we know that they
10. (go)

_____ a lifetime of happiness after they _____ married next month.
11. (have)   12. (get)

So, what _____ during the next 10 years? What careers will we be working in?
13. (we / all / do)

How will we do as spouses and parents? Stay in touch, and come to our 10-year class reunion. By

that time, we _____ or _____ for 10 years. Many of us _____
14. (work)   15. (study)   16. (become)

parents by then, and we certainly _____ a lot to talk about on that reunion night in 10
17. (have)

years!

6 | EDITING

Read the text of an e-mail from Marco, an international student studying in the United States, to Ricardo, his friend back home. There are 19 mistakes in the use of verb forms. The first mistake is already corrected. Find and correct 18 more.

Dear Ricardo:

    have been
    I ~~am~~ here in the United States for two months now, and my English is already improving.

I'm writing to you in English so we can both get more practice. Classes in my intensive English

program in Chicago are going on for about six weeks. The instructors has given homework every

day, and I have been studying a lot. In fact, I study right now because I have a big test tomorrow.

    Even more than in class, I have learn a great deal of English by talking with people in the city.

In my apartment building, most people are speaking English, and when I need something, I speak

to the manager in English. For example, the plumbing in my apartment often doesn't work, and

I'm explaining the problem to the manager several times already. The plumber is coming next

Tuesday, again. In fact, the same plumber is coming every week!

On the negative side, the weather has been quite bad this month. It's raining almost every day. In addition, sometimes I feel lonely. I don't meet many friendly people so far, and I'm not having any fun since I got here. So, please write to me soon! I always feel good when I hear from you.

I'm very happy when I'll come home again next year. When I will leave here, I will had been studying English for a year and, hopefully, will have learn a lot. By this time next year I have finished my studies forever, and I'll work with my dad in his office. With luck I learn English well while I'm here, and that will be helpful in Dad's business.

Your friend,

Marco

7 | PERSONALIZATION

Write about your life. Use some of the phrases in the box.

So far, my life . . .	In fact, next week . . .
Since I graduated from high school, . . .	At the end of next year, . . .
For the past two years, . . .	By the end of next year, . . .
Right now . . .	In 10 years, . . .
Very soon, . . .	By the time I am old, . . .

_____

_____

_____

_____

_____

_____

_____

_____

_____

_____

2 Past Time

1 | USING VERB FORMS

Read this passage and table about world population. Complete the passage. Circle the correct verb forms.

How many people (have ever lived)/ had ever lived on
1.
earth? It is impossible to know that, but demographers have

attempted to estimate this figure. They based their estimates

on an assumption that humans first have lived / lived on earth
2.
in the year 50,000 B.C. The demographers also guessed the

average size of the human population at different periods.

At the dawn of agriculture, about 8000 B.C., about 5

million people have been living / were living in the entire
3.
world. That is about the population of the city of Baghdad

today, or of the whole country of Denmark.

YEAR	POPULATION
50,000 B.C.	2
8000 B.C.	5,000,000
A.D. 1	300,000,000
1200	450,000,000
1650	500,000,000
1750	795,000,000
1850	1,265,000,000
1900	1,656,000,000
1950	2,516,000,000
1995	5,760,000,000
2002	6,215,000,000

Over the years, populations in different regions were / would increase or decline in response
4.
to famines, the condition of cattle herds, hostilities between people, and changing weather and

climate. High mortality from these factors offset the high birth rates. People's life spans

used to be / are very short; statistically, life expectancy at birth probably averaged only about 10
5.
years throughout most of human history. Today, in contrast, it is about 57 years, worldwide, and

as much as 80 in some countries.

The population of the entire world <u>would be / was</u> about 300 million in A.D. 1—about the
6.
size of the United States today—according to one estimate. By 1650, the entire world population

<u>had risen / was rising</u> to about 500 million, or about 8 percent of what it is today. The population
7.
<u>had been growing / has grown</u> more slowly for several hundred years before that due to the
8.
tremendous toll of the plague, or Black Death. By 1800, however, the world population had

passed the 1 billion mark, and it <u>had continued / continued</u> to grow. Populations
9.
<u>were benefitting / used to benefit</u> from better hygiene and public sanitation, more widely
10.
available food supplies, improved nutrition, and, more recently, vastly improved medicine.

In the 1990s, demographers predicted that early in the 21st century, the population of the world

<u>reaches / would reach</u> 6 billion. They were right: in 2002, the population of the world
11.
<u>had reached / reached</u> 6 billion.
12.
Using certain assumptions, statisticians have estimated that about 106 billion people

<u>have lived / have been living</u> since the beginning of the human race. And about 5.8 percent of all
13.
the people ever born are alive today.

2 | ORDERING ACTIONS IN PAST TIME

*This morning Professor Harry Williams called the police to report that an intruder had
entered his house during the night. When the police arrived, he told them this story. In each
set of sentences, write* **1** *in front of the action that happened first and* **2** *in front of
the action that happened second. If the actions happened at the same time, write* **S** *on
both lines.*

1. When I got up this morning, I found that a large glass door had been broken during the night.

   __2__ Harry got up.

   __1__ A door had been broken.

2. It appeared that a thief had entered the house while I was sleeping.

   _____ A thief had entered the house.

   _____ He was sleeping.

3. I looked around the house and found that the drawers of my desk were open.

   _____ He found the drawers open.

   _____ He looked around the house.

(continued)

4. Worriedly, I ran to my desk and discovered that my passport was missing.

_____ He ran to his desk.

_____ He discovered that his passport was missing.

5. After I searched further, I realized that my keys were gone, too.

_____ He realized that his keys were gone.

_____ He searched further.

6. As I was dialing the police, someone rang the bell.

_____ He was dialing the police.

_____ Someone rang the bell.

7. When I opened the door, I saw my neighbor. He smiled and handed me my keys.

_____ Harry opened the door.

_____ His neighbor handed him his keys.

8. "I found these on the sidewalk," my neighbor said. "Thank you so much," I said. "And by the way, have you seen my passport?" I asked. "Your passport?" he answered, "No. You told me you had sent it in for renewal."

_____ Harry told the neighbor about his passport.

_____ Harry sent in his passport for renewal.

9. "Oh, right! I did! I completely forgot," I said. "I suspected that someone had stolen it, along with my keys."

_____ Harry suspected something.

_____ Someone stole his passport and keys (he believed).

10. "Oh, Harry! You've done it again! You are a totally absent-minded professor!" he said. I smiled. "I guess I am. Won't you come in?" I asked my neighbor.

_____ Harry smiled.

_____ He invited his neighbor into the house.

3 | USING VERB FORMS

Read this passage from a memoir. Complete the passage. Circle the correct verb forms.

My parents and I came to live in the United States when I was five years old. We

(had thought) / were thinking that everybody in America was very rich. Imagine our surprise when
    1.

we learned / were learning that it was very difficult for many people, my father included, to make
    2.

a living.

My father had been working / has been working as a dentist in Europe before we
          3.

have come / came here 31 years ago. Here he couldn't work as a dentist right away because he
  4.

hadn't been passing / hadn't passed the state examinations yet. While he had studied / was studying
    5.   **6.**

for the dentist examinations, he <u>worked / had worked</u> in a dental laboratory in order to support
                                        7.

his family.

Within a year, he <u>was passing / had passed</u> the examinations and <u>established / used to</u>
                            8.   **9.**

<u>establish</u> himself in a practice with a local dentist. He had a long and successful career as a dentist.

By the time he <u>retired / was retiring</u> last year, he <u>was practicing / had been practicing</u> dentistry here
                    10.   **11.**

for 30 years. During his career, he earned the respect of his peers and the devotion of his patients,

as well as the love of the poor immigrants to whom he <u>used to contribute / was contributing</u> his
                                                            12.

services free of charge.

My mother, too, <u>has been / had been</u> happy here. She <u>got / has gotten</u> a degree in finance five
                    13.   **14.**

years ago, and she now owns and operates her own profitable copy center. She <u>has been taking /</u>
                                                                                    15.

<u>had been taking</u> courses for a long time before she actually <u>got / had gotten</u> her degree. She <u>would</u>
                                                                    16.

<u>take / has taken</u> only one or two courses each semester because she was busy looking after my
    17.

father, my brother, and me. Now she is an independent woman who runs her own business.

I myself <u>have been having / had had</u> a wonderful life. Three years ago I <u>got / had gotten</u> my
                18.   **19.**

law degree, and since then I <u>have been working / was working</u> in a small law firm where I am very
                                20.

happy. I know the partners of the firm quite well, as I <u>used to work / was working</u> here in the
                                                            21.

summers when I was in law school. While I <u>worked / was working</u> here one summer, I <u>met / was</u>
                                            22.   **23.**

<u>meeting</u> a terrific man, whom I married the following year. He doesn't work here anymore; he <u>was</u>

<u>becoming / became</u> a judge and is well respected in the community.
        24.

My family and I faced some difficulties when we first <u>arrived / were arriving</u> in this country
                                                            25.

because we <u>hadn't expected / haven't expected</u> things to be as difficult as they in fact were. We
                26.

didn't know then what we know now: that we <u>used to succeed / would succeed</u> beyond our
                                                27.

wildest dreams.

4 | USING VERB FORMS

*This conversation between Al Albert (**A**) and Bob Bradley (**B**) occurs at Beautiville Central High School's 10-year reunion. Circle the letter of the phrase that completes each sentence correctly.*

1. **A:** Hi, Bob! Great to see you!

   B: Great to see you, too, Al. What _____ for these past ten years?

   a. did you do   **c.** have you been doing

   b. have you done   **d.** had you done

2. **A:** Well, I'm a doctor. I _____ a pediatrics office last month.

   a. have just opened   **c.** was just opening

   b. just opened   **d.** had just opened

3. **B:** Oh, a doctor! I thought you _____ law.

   a. study   **c.** are studying

   b. have studied   **d.** were studying

4. **A:** You have a good memory. I _____ law, but I decided to go into medicine instead.

   a. studied   **c.** would study

   b. have studied   **d.** was going to study

5. **A:** What about you?

   B: I write TV scripts. I _____ in advertising until Comic Productions _____ me a job last year.

   a. had been working / offered   **c.** have worked / offered

   b. worked / had offered   **d.** worked / had been offering

6. **A:** Well, you always were very funny. I remember that you _____ the funniest guy in our class. Whenever you made a joke, everybody _____ laugh so much.

   a. had been / used to   **c.** would be / used to

   b. used to be / would   **d.** have been / was laughing

   B: Aw, gee.

7. **B:** By the way, do you remember Jenny James? She writes, too. In fact, her first novel _____.
Finally!

    a. just came out   **c.** was just coming

    b. had just come out   **d.** had just been coming out

    A: Finally?

8. **A:** Yes. By the time Brown-Smith Publishing _____ it, 11 other publishers _____ it.

    a. had accepted / had rejected   **c.** accepted / had rejected

    b. accepted / rejected   **d.** had accepted / rejected it

    B: Oh, wow.

9. **A:** Now, tell me about you and Rose. Do you have any children?

    B: Oh, Rose and I _____ married for only two years. We split up.

    a. have been   **c.** used to be

    b. were   **d.** would be

10. **A:** You _____ divorced from Rose? You and Rose, the class sweethearts? I'm sorry.

    a. get   **c.** were getting

    b. got   **d.** had been getting

    B: Well, thank you.

11. **A:** We should get together sometime and talk about our carefree past.

    B: Right. Our carefree past. Do you remember how our biggest concern _____ whether or not we _____ a date on Saturday night?

    a. had been / used to have   **c.** would be / used to have

    b. used to be / would have   **d.** was / have had

12. **B:** I sure do. Those _____ the good old days.

    a. were   **c.** had been

    b. have been   **d.** would be

5 | USING VERB FORMS

Read this entry from Lila's diary, in which she is complaining about her husband, Craig.
Complete the entry. Use the words or phrases in the box.

buy	call	~~cut~~	didn't	fix
has	hasn't	is	making	promises
take	was going to	will		

July 22nd

Promises! Promises! I'll never believe another thing that Craig tells me.
Last week he told me that he would _____cut_____ the grass, but he hasn't
                                          1.
done it yet. Then he said that he was going to _____ the leaky
                                                      2.
faucet in the kitchen, but it _____ still dripping.
                                    3.

He promised that he would _____ my mom to wish her a happy
                                    4.
birthday, but he _____ done that, either. He thinks I'll feel better if
                        5.
he _____ to buy me an expensive gift. He told me that he was going
        6.
to _____ me a big surprise on Valentine's Day, but he
        7.
_____ even give me a card.
        8.

Our anniversary is next month, and he said that he was _____
                                                                9.
reservations at a fancy hotel to spend the weekend, but I'll bet that he
_____ forgotten all about it. He even promised that he
        10.
_____ give me a car for my birthday, but he didn't say which
        11.
birthday.

There is one thing I know that he will do: nap. He told me that he would
_____ a nap this afternoon, and I'm sure that he _____
        12.   13.
take one!

6 | USING VERB FORMS

Read this newspaper article about a special anniversary. Complete the article by writing the correct forms of the verbs in parentheses.

Anniversary Celebration Held

A second wedding anniversary celebration was held in the Downtown Center Hotel last night for Helena K. Messenger and Julius Lister. A group of 250 people, including the couple's eight children, were in attendance. The story of how these two amazing people met so late in their lives is most interesting.

Helena K. Messenger is anything but a stereotypical senior citizen. Her hair is naturally black and curly, and she drives very, very fast, zooming up her long driveway like a teenager. She _____*runs*_____ a mile every day,
1. (run)
takes aerobic exercise classes, and appears to have none of the usual fears that come with age: Neither extra-spicy food nor loneliness concern her at all.

After her first husband _____
2. (die)
in 1993, she _____ living in their
3. (continue)
big, creaky house in New Jersey, surrounded by quiet, empty rooms. In 2000, while she

_____ a singles discussion group,
4. (attend)
someone _____ her to Julius Lister.
5. (introduce)
Mr. Lister works full time as an engineer in one of the army's research centers. He has several

hobbies, including windsurfing, canoeing, and hiking. Mr. Lister _____ his first
6. (lose)
wife in 1999, and just before he

_____ Ms. Messenger he
7. (meet)
_____ dating again, without
8. (begin)
much success. One of his daughters recalled,

"He _____ out with women
9. (go)
from time to time, but he said it was very depressing."

After the meeting, Ms. Messenger

_____ Mr. Lister a postcard
10. (send)
saying that she _____ to see him
11. (like)
again. As soon as he _____ the
12. (receive)
postcard, he _____ and
13. (call)
_____ her to dinner. The rest is
14. (invite)
history. Since then, they _____
15. (spend)
almost all of their time together. They

_____ to many parts of the
16. (travel)
world during the past two years. When they married, they expected to enjoy life more than

they _____ it in the past, but
17. (enjoy)
neither one expected to be enjoying it so completely. Much to everyone's delight, they are indeed living happily ever after.

7 | EDITING

Read this passage about Albert Einstein. There are 19 mistakes in the use of verbs referring to the past time. The first mistake is already corrected. Find and correct 18 more.

Albert Einstein, one of the world's most renowned scientists, was born in Germany in 1879. It

                 didn't talk

is said that he ~~wasn't talking~~ until he was four years old, and that his parents and others believed

that he was of average intelligence, or less. When he was in elementary school, his teachers hadn't

thought he was a promising student. By the time he was eight years old, they have already decided

that he could not learn as fast as his classmates could. Furthermore, he didn't had much interest in

his classes, and he will not give time to studying the required Latin and Greek.

The only subject that interested him was mathematics. However, even this interest caused

trouble with his teachers; Einstein has been solving mathematical problems in his own way, which

was different from the way of the prescribed curriculum. His teachers don't believe that his future

will be very bright.

When Einstein was 16, he left school. His parents were moving to Italy earlier, so he decided

to follow them there. After he is in Italy for only a few months, he decided to enter another

school, the Zurich Polytechnic, in Switzerland. When he arrived there, he encountered other

problems: The teachers forced him to study the same subjects that the other students study at the

time. Of course, he already mastered the basic subjects that were taught in the school, and so he

quickly had become bored and disillusioned. He has been studying physics and other natural

sciences by himself before that time, and he had always hoped to continue in his own way. After

many frustrations, he finally has graduated from the Polytechnic just after he turned 21 years old.

At that time, he began publishing his important scientific theories. At first, his theories weren't

accepted, but after a while, other scientists were realizing how brilliant they were, and Einstein

received the recognition he deserved.

Einstein settled in the United States before World War II. He taught at Princeton University in

New Jersey, and continued to make important contributions to science. In the town of Princeton,

he used to walking around town like any ordinary citizen, and he was usually not recognized as

the great man that he was.

Einstein's theories changed the ways that scientists were thinking about time, space, and matter. His ideas, such as the theory of relativity, continue to be valid today. There has been no other scientist of such importance in the 20th century, and indeed, he is among the few great scientists of all time.

8 | PERSONALIZATION

Write a brief history of the life of one of your parents. Use some of the phrases in the box.

> When my father (mother) was born, his (her) family . . .
> While he (she) was in school, . . .
> Before finishing school, . . .
> After finishing school, . . .
> His (her) first job . . .
> He (she) met my mother (father) . . .
> Before I was born, . . .
> When I was born, . . .
> After I started school, . . .
> As a parent, . . .
> In 2002, . . .
> Since last year, . . .
> These days, . . .

_____

_____

_____

_____

_____

_____

_____

_____

Simple and Progressive: Action and Non-Action Verbs

1 | RECOGNIZING NON-ACTION VERBS

Read this letter to a newspaper editor. A citizen is stating his case for higher taxes. There are 14 non-action verbs. The first one is already underlined. Find and underline 13 more.

Dear Editor:

We <u>need</u> higher taxes in this town. Probably nobody believes me, but this is true. Nobody wants to pay more money, but everybody desires more services and a better quality of life. I know that these things are true:

1. We don't have enough police officers. More police officers mean safer streets and safer neighborhoods.
2. We love our children, and we want a good education for them. However, it doesn't appear that we are going to get the smaller classes, pre-kindergarten classes, and proper student advising that our young people deserve.
3. We drive on some roads that are in bad condition and are badly lighted. Please fix the roads and put up more and better lighting.

We owe it to ourselves and our children to maintain and improve our community. When our citizens understand the value of their tax contributions, they will not mind paying a little more now toward a better future.

Sincerely yours,
Jonathan Jeffries

2 | USING ACTION AND NON-ACTION VERBS

ZXQ Marketing is taking a survey on the street to find out which technological device people use the most. Read this excerpt from the survey. Complete the sentences by writing the correct forms—simple present or present progressive—of the verbs in parentheses.

ZXQ: Good morning! Hello, there! Thank you for stopping to talk to us. We

_____*are taking*_____ a survey of people passing by. Could you please tell us
<u>1. (take)</u>

what the most important modern device in your everyday life is, sir?

MAN #1: Oh, that's easy. Everybody _____ the computer is the most
<u>2. (know)</u>

important.

ZXQ: Well, a lot of people _____ with that! What about you, ma'am?
<u>3. (agree)</u>

WOMAN #1: I _____ computers, and I _____ one. I really
<u>4. (not / understand)</u>   <u>5. (not / use)</u>

_____ my cell phone, though. Listen! It _____
<u>6. (need)</u>   <u>7. (ring)</u>

now! Someone _____ me at this very moment.
<u>8. (call)</u>

ZXQ: Yes, a cell phone is vital to many people. Now, you, sir?

MAN #2: Well, I _____ a difficult time these days since my eyes aren't so
<u>9. (have)</u>

good any more. I _____ well enough to read. But I
<u>10. (not see)</u>

_____ television very well, and I _____
<u>11. (see)</u>   <u>12. (hear)</u>

perfectly. So, for me, television is the most important of the modern inventions.

Actually, I _____ a lot now that I never knew before from the
<u>13. (learn)</u>

science programs and the political programs.

ZXQ: Yes, indeed, television has changed the world. Now, one more opinion. Miss?

WOMAN #2: Ever since I got my new job, I _____ time to cook. I really
<u>14. (not / have)</u>

_____ my microwave. I _____ entire dinners
<u>15. (appreciate)</u>   <u>16. (cook)</u>

in about 15 minutes. As a matter of fact, my boss _____ to
<u>17. (come)</u>

dinner tonight, and I _____ a wonderful fish-and-vegetable dish
<u>18. (make)</u>

in the microwave. With mangoes and tomatoes and ginger. . . .

ZXQ: Mmm! That sure _____ good! Well, thank you, ladies and
<u>19. (sound)</u>

gentlemen.

3 | USING ADVERBS OR ADJECTIVES

Complete the sentences. Circle the correct adjectives or adverbs.

1. My accountant's calculations don't seem very (exact)/ exactly. I am going to find a new accountant.

2. The jeweler measured the diamond very closely and then found the perfect setting for it; the diamond fit the new setting exact / exactly.

3. The diamond looks beautiful / beautifully in its new setting.

4. Hmmm . . . this problem seems very hard / hardly. I don't think that I can solve it.

5. The student answered the difficult math problem correct / correctly in just a few minutes.

6. This soup tastes delicious / deliciously! What did you put in it?

7. The baby tasted the cereal quick / quickly and then spit it all out.

8. Uh oh—this noise doesn't sound good / well. I'm going to pull over and take a look at the engine.

9. You look very sad / sadly today. Is something the matter?

10. Domingo sings very well / good. He hopes to become an opera singer.

11. When we invited Barbara to join us after the concert, she replied "Sorry, I'm going home now. I'm feeling really tired / tiredly."

12. It's taking a long time for the show to begin. The children are acting impatient / impatiently.

13. The teacher answered the question patient / patiently. As a result, Gina gained more confidence and began to feel good / well about herself.

14. The meaning of this sentence does not seem clear / clearly. If you use commas, it means one thing; if you don't use commas, it means something else. Please punctuate clear / clearly.

4 | EDITING

*Read this conversation between a lifeguard (**A**) and a surfer (**B**). There are 13 mistakes in verb forms or in the use of adjectives and adverbs. The first mistake is already corrected. Find and correct 12 more.*

A: Hey, there! Come back! Don't go in the water!

B: Huh? What's the matter?

A: The beach is closed. Sharks are in the area today.

B: Aw, I'm having fun. ~~I'm not seeing~~ *I don't see* any sharks!

A: It doesn't matter. It doesn't look dangerously out there, but it is.

B: OK. OK. Gee—I've been surfing for years, and I've never been seeing a shark in this area! I feel very safely here.

A: Well, we're having reports that there's sharks in the water today—lots of them. They're congregating around that reef, right over there. Sharks especially like surfers, didn't you know that?

B: No way!

A: It's true.

B: Are you meaning that surfers have something special that attracts sharks?

A: Not exactly. When a shark sees a person on a surfboard—especially on a short surfboard—he is thinking that it's a seal. The outline of the surfer from below the surface of the water looks like a seal.

B: You sound seriously.

(continued)

A: I am serious. Listen to me.

B: I am listening. I'm hearing you very good, but I'm not sure I believe you!

A: Well, believe it. The sharks are behaving very aggressive today, and I want all the swimmers and surfers to be safe. You can't be too carefully, you know.

5 | PERSONALIZATION

Write two or three paragraphs about what you think is necessary for a happy and fulfilling life. Use as many of the phrases in the box as possible.

I (don't) think . . .	I (don't) have . . .
I (don't) need . . .	I've been having . . .
I (don't) want . . .	I (don't) know . . .
I love . . .	I (don't) believe . . .
I've been thinking about . . .	There seems (doesn't seem) . . .
I (don't) remember . . .	

_____

_____

_____

_____

_____

_____

_____

_____

_____

_____

_____

_____

_____

_____

_____

Be and Auxiliaries in Additions, Tags, and Short Answers

1 | RECOGNIZING AUXILIARIES

Read the text of an e-mail from Rachel to Marilyn. There are 14 phrases with a form of **be** *or an auxiliary construction that is used to show similarity, contrast, or emphasis. The first phrase is already underlined. Find and underline 13 more.*

Hello Marilyn,

    <u>I do hope</u> we get to see you on our vacation next summer, but here's the thing: Sam and I can't agree on where to spend our next summer's vacation.

    As usual, he wants to spend time in the wilderness, <u>but I don't</u>. He enjoys hiking in the woods and going kayaking, <u>but I don't</u>. Some people are city people. <u>I am</u>, and <u>I do</u> like to visit new cities all over the world. I like to wander along new streets and visit historic places, <u>but he doesn't</u>.

    Sometimes I wonder how we got together! And how we stay together. <u>But</u>, really, <u>I do</u> know that. He loves the idea of family and togetherness, and <u>I do</u> too. He doesn't like to party much, and <u>neither do I</u>. I prefer cozy weekends at home, and <u>so does he</u>. I can't stay awake past 10:00 P.M. and <u>he can't either</u>. When we first met, I knew immediately that we would be together forever, and <u>so did he</u>.

    So, to make a long story short: Hopefully, we will see you. It's not certain, <u>but it *is*</u> possible that we will be coming through Chicago on our way someplace. <u>We do</u> want to spend at least one day with you.

See you soon, I hope.

—Rachel

2 | USING AUXILIARIES

Using the information about chimpanzees and gorillas in the chart, complete each sentence below with the appropriate auxiliary, or with the auxiliary and **so**, **too**, **either**, *or* **neither***. Use a separate word for each blank space. Use contractions if appropriate.*

Chimpanzees

- Are native to western and central Africa
- Live in groups
- Walk on all fours, resting their upper body on their knuckles
- Are excitable
- Are mainly vegetarian, but do hunt and eat some smaller animals
- Can devise primitive tools
- A few can use a type of sign language
- May live up to 50 years

Gorillas

- Are native to western and central Africa
- Live in groups
- Walk on all fours, resting their upper body on their knuckles
- Are gentle and calm
- Are totally vegetarian

- Cannot devise primitive tools
- None can use a type of sign language
- May live more than 40 years

1. Chimpanzees are found in central and western Africa, and gorillas _____*are*_____ _____*too*_____.

2. Chimpanzees and gorillas are similar in several ways. In the wild, chimpanzees live together in groups, and gorillas __*do too*__ _____.

3. Chimpanzees walk on all fours, resting their upper body on their knuckles, and _____*so*_____ _____*do*_____ gorillas.

4. In other ways, chimpanzees and gorillas are different. Chimpanzees are excitable, but gorillas __*aren't*_____; gorillas are calmer than chimpanzees.

5. Chimpanzees eat smaller animals, but gorillas _____; they are totally vegetarian.

6. Chimpanzees can actually devise primitive tools, but gorillas __can't__ .

7. For example, a chimpanzee uses a stick to collect insects from holes and stones, but a gorilla __doesn't__ .

8. The gorilla doesn't know how to use a stick; however, the chimpanzee __does__ .

9. Chimpanzees don't use speech as humans do, and __neither__ __do__ gorillas. However, a few chimpanzees in captivity have been taught to communicate some concepts using a kind of sign language.

10. In good circumstances, chimpanzees can live into their 40s, and __so__ __can__ gorillas.

3 | USING *BE* AND *DO* FOR CONTRAST WHERE POSSIBLE

Complete the following statements with the appropriate verb forms for contrast. Use auxiliary verbs or a form of **be**.

1. Ponce de León didn't discover the fountain of youth that he was looking for, but he __did discover__ Florida.

2. Even though many of the early American settlers didn't survive the first year in Massachusetts, about half of them __did__ ; these settlers celebrated the first Thanksgiving with the local Native Americans.

3. Alaska is not the most populous state in the United States, but it __is__ the largest in area.

4. A lot of people don't eat as much meat as they used to, but they __eat__ more fish.

5. Not all eligible citizens vote in elections, but many __do vote__ .

6. Some adults don't know how to use text messaging or DVDs, but a lot of teenagers __do know__ how to use these things.

7. Guglielmo Marconi was not the inventor of the telephone, but he __was__ the inventor of the telegraph.

8. Even though dogs and cats don't understand the words people speak to them, they __do understand__ when people are angry at them.

9. The North Pole doesn't have penguins, but it __does have__ polar bears.

4 | USING SHORT ANSWERS

Using the information in the graph, match the questions on the left with the correct answers on the right.

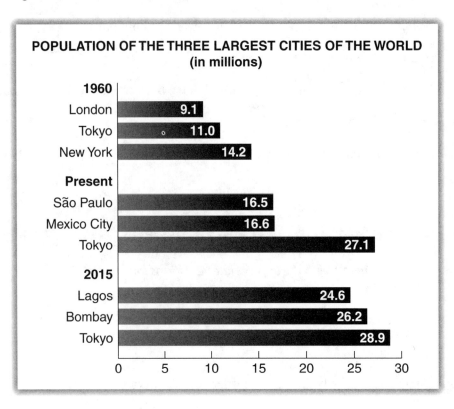

POPULATION OF THE THREE LARGEST CITIES OF THE WORLD
(in millions)

1960
London — 9.1
Tokyo — 11.0
New York — 14.2

Present
São Paulo — 16.5
Mexico City — 16.6
Tokyo — 27.1

2015
Lagos — 24.6
Bombay — 26.2
Tokyo — 28.9

_c_ 1. Was New York the largest city in 1960?

_h_ 2. Has Tokyo been one of the three largest cities since 1960?

_k_ 3. Will Tokyo be one of the largest cities in 2015?

_j_ 4. Will Bombay and Lagos be among the largest cities in 2015?

_a_ 5. Does São Paulo have as many people as Tokyo?

_i_ 6. Is London still among the most populous cities of the world?

_g_ 7. Will New York be among the most populous cities of the world in 2015?

_b_ 8. Have Los Angeles and Buenos Aires ever been among the three most populous cities of the world?

_d_ 9. Did Lagos appear among the three most populous cities of the world in 1960?

_l_ 10. Did São Paulo and Mexico City appear among the most populous cities of the world in 1960?

a. No, it doesn't.

b. No, they haven't.

c. ~~Yes, it was.~~

d. No, it didn't.

e. Yes, they do.

f. Yes, there are.

g. No, it won't.

h. Yes, it has.

i. No, it's not.

j. Yes, they will.

k. Yes, it will.

l. No, they didn't.

e **11.** Do 16 million people or more live in Mexico City?

f **12.** Are there more than 27 million people living in Tokyo?

5 | FORMING TAG QUESTIONS

Read this passage from a court report. Complete the passage by adding tag questions to the attorney's statements to the witness.

> On the night of June 24, Harry Norton disappeared. He had been at home having dinner with his wife and two friends when he received a phone call. He was on the phone for about two minutes, and then left home abruptly, saying that he would return in 15 minutes. He never returned, and no one has heard from him since then. The police suspect foul play. The district attorney is interrogating a witness, one of the dinner guests, now.

1. You were in Norton's house on the night of June 24, _____ *weren't you* _____?

2. You heard Norton on the phone, _____ *didn't you* _____?

3. You weren't able to understand the topic of the conversation, _____ *were you* _____?

4. Norton didn't seem upset, _____ *did he* _____?

5. The conversation took about two minutes, _____ *didn't it* _____?

6. Now, you've known Harry Norton a long time, _____ *haven't you* _____?

7. You've never had a serious argument or a falling out, _____ *have you* _____?

8. So, Harry Norton would tell you if he was in trouble, _____ *wouldn't he* _____?

9. As far as you know, Harry Norton wasn't in any trouble, _____ *was he* _____?

10. And, you don't know why he went out or where he went, _____ *do you* _____?

6 | USING ADDITIONS THAT REFER TO PRECEDING INFORMATION

Complete the conversations. Use the phrases in the box.

I already have	I know you can	I'm sure it will	~~It is~~	It isn't	They say it is

1. **A:** I suppose you think my idea is crazy!

   B: _____ *It is* _____! Nobody's going to believe that!

2. **A:** This looks like the right road.

   B: _____ *It isn't* _____! Don't turn here!

(continued)

3. **A:** I'm not sure whether this plan will succeed or not.

   B: *I am sure it will* . Let's go for it.

4. **A:** I don't think I can meet the deadline, boss.

   B: _____. Just work late this week.

5. **A:** The doctor will see you soon. But first you have to fill out these forms, and . . .

   B: _____.

6. **A:** Is the plane on time today?

   B: *They say it is* _____, but it's always late.

7 | EDITING

Read this passage from a lecture on planets. There are 11 mistakes in the use of auxiliary verbs. The first mistake is already corrected. Find and correct 10 more.

Some scientists have called Earth and Venus "twin planets" since they are the most similar of any two planets in the solar system. Relatively speaking, Earth is close to the sun, and Venus ~~does~~ *is*, too. They are similar, too, in size, mass, density, and volume. Both planets are "young" in terms of the universe: Earth formed about 4 or 5 billion years ago, and Venus has *did*, too. Earth's landscapes were formed by rain, water, sea, wind, earthquakes, and volcanoes; Venus's landscapes have *were* too. In fact, Earth's surface is still being formed by volcanoes; it is possible that Venus's was *is*, too, even though missions to Venus have not shown any active volcanoes.

On the other hand, there are remarkable differences between the planets. Most significantly, Earth supports life, but Venus does *n't*. First, it is too hot on Venus to support life. The average temperature on Earth is about 22°C, but on Venus it is 480°C. Second, Venus's atmosphere contains carbon dioxide, a poisonous gas; so do *es* Earth's atmosphere, although so far the carbon dioxide level from pollution has not reached lethal levels. Then, Earth has oceans, but Venus don't *does not have*.

Strangely, Venus rotates from east to west, but the other planets aren't *don't*; they rotate from west to east. Furthermore, Earth completes a day in 24 hours, but Venus don't *does not*. It takes 243 Earth days for Venus to make a total rotation.

It's interesting, doesn't *isn't* it, that two planets so similar are also so different? You'll be able to see Venus as it crosses the face of the sun in the next Transit of Venus, which will be in 2012. Will we be watching? I know we are *will*!

8 | PERSONALIZATION

A Your best friend agrees with you about most things. Write a paragraph about the similarities you share. Use the auxiliaries in the box.

he (she) . . . , too	neither . . . she (he)
he (she) . . . , not either	so . . . she (he)

_____

_____

_____

_____

_____

_____

_____

_____

B You have a relative that you love, even though you disagree on many things. Write a paragraph about your differences. Use the phrases in the box.

. . . but I do.	. . . but I don't.	. . . but I am.	. . . but I'm not.

_____

_____

_____

_____

_____

_____

_____

_____

UNIT 5

Modals to Express Degrees of Necessity

1 | USING MODAL EXPRESSIONS OF NECESSITY

Read this flyer about The FitNiche, a place where people go to become healthier and stronger. Complete the passage. Circle the correct modals or modal-like expressions.

The FitNiche

People who want to benefit from our program (must not)/ don't have to eat junk food. In
1.
order to benefit, they should / might eat only the food prescribed by The FitNiche. This food
2.
is tasty; contrary to what many people think, healthy food doesn't have to / must not taste
3.
terrible. We think that our participants should / have got to take a vitamin–mineral supplement, too, to
4.
ensure getting all the necessary nutrition; however, people who are sure they are eating properly
don't have to / must not take supplements.
5.

The program has certain strict rules about exercise: Participants have to / should exercise at least
6.
three times a week and must / could exercise for at least 30 minutes each time. In fact, participants
7.
should / had better exercise five times a week if possible, even though this is not a program requirement.
8.

In addition, The FitNiche offers yoga, meditation, tai chi, and life coaching for those who want the benefits
from such disciplines. There is no extra charge for these activities, and if you have any interest at all in them,
you ought to / had better take this opportunity to give them a try.
9.

Finally, all members are closely monitored by our professional staff. We speak with you each time that you
come, in order to find out how you are progressing in the program. If you had to / were supposed to exercise
10.
but you didn't have the time, we'll adjust the exercise program to fit your schedule better.

Remember that The FitNiche wants you to be healthy and to enjoy getting healthy. At the end of our
program, you will say, "I had to change / should have changed my habits, and I did! It wasn't difficult at all.
11.
Now I'm going to stay healthy, thanks to The FitNiche. I should have / had better come here much sooner."
12.

30

2 | USING MODAL EXPRESSIONS OF NECESSITY

Read these conversations between employees in an office. Circle the letter of the word or phrase that completes each sentence correctly.

1. **A:** You weren't at the office picnic, Blanca. How come?

   B: Oh, I didn't have a ride. My sister _____ me there and come with me, but she never came to my house. Her car had a dead battery.

   a. drove   **b.** was supposed to drive   **c.** had to drive

2. **A:** Did you finish that report last night, Mike?

   B: No, I didn't. I _____ late, but I went home instead.

   a. had to work   **b.** should have worked   **c.** worked

3. **A:** Were you sick yesterday, Bob?

   B: Yes, I was. I _____ to the doctor. That's why I didn't come to work.

   a. should have gone   **b.** was supposed to go   **c.** had to go

4. **A:** Sacha, why weren't you at the meeting this morning?

   B: Oh, but I _____ at the meeting. I came in late and sat in the back.

   a. should have been   **b.** had to be   **c.** was

5. **A:** Ken, why weren't you at the meeting this morning?

   B: I'm sorry. I _____ there, but I got to work late today.

   a. had to be   **b.** should have been   **c.** was

6. **A:** Did you call Elizabeth to remind her of the meeting?

   B: I _____ her. She just called to remind me!

   a. didn't have to call   **b.** should have called   **c.** have got to call

(continued)

7. **A:** How come we _____ heat up our lunches in the microwave anymore?

   B: Everybody was complaining about the food odors, so the boss just said, "No more cooking in the office kitchen."

   a. had better not   **b.** aren't allowed to   **c.** don't have to

8. **A:** Can you help me with my computer, Kim? It crashed again.

   B: I can't right now, Henry. I _____ fix Sally's machine. It's an emergency. I'll come down later, OK?

   a. should   **b.** have got to   **c.** I had to

9. **A:** Attendance at the annual HR meeting is mandatory. Everyone _____ attend.

   B: Oh, gee. I was hoping to take the afternoon off.

   a. should   **b.** must   **c.** is allowed to

10. **A:** Going to lunch with us today, Sam?

    B: Hmmm . . . _____. I have too much work to do.

    a. I'd better not   **b.** I don't have to   **c.** I'm not supposed to

3 | USING MODAL EXPRESSIONS OF NECESSITY

Read this memorandum. Cross out the modals and modal-like expressions in this memorandum that are NOT appropriate in the sentences. Cross out either one or two items in each underlined set.

MEMORANDUM

To: All Sales Associates
From: Syd Miles, Sales Director
Subject: Downturn

I know we've all worked hard this year to sell our product. In spite of everyone's efforts, though, sales are down 9.2 percent for the year. We all must / ~~ought to~~ / have got to work
1.
harder now to make our company profitable. It's absolutely necessary, or the company can't survive. We are ~~supposed to do~~ / ~~should have done~~ / have to do several essential things,
2.
starting right now. Actually, we should have made / must make / ~~had to make~~ these changes
3.
a year ago, but unfortunately we didn't.

First, we must ~~have~~ / ~~could~~ / must cut down on our overhead costs. Management
4.
had considered eliminating about 10 positions, but so far they
aren't supposed to / aren't allowed to / haven't had to lay off anybody. Instead,
5.
management says that we all had better / should / have to take a mandatory 10 percent pay
6.
cut for this year. But, if sales go up, everyone will get a nice bonus, and salaries will go up
15 percent for next year.

We all had better / have got to / ~~should have~~ cut down on expenses, or we won't make it.
7.
This means that there will be less travel, and nobody is ~~supposed~~ to / is allowed to / ~~has to~~
8.
take family along on sales trips anymore. Lunches and dinners at company expense will be
few and far between. We ~~must not~~ / don't have to / ~~aren't allowed to~~ entertain clients at
9.
meals; it's not necessary. We can transact our business in our offices or by phone, fax, and
e-mail. Also, please be careful of company supplies. Try not to waste paper in the printer,
and don't use the company phone to make your own long-distance phone calls. Even though
we all know that we are ~~not to~~ / ~~don't have~~ to / shouldn't use the phone for personal calls,
10.
the rule has not been enforced. But it will be now.

Thank you for your understanding and cooperation. We'll meet on Monday to discuss this
further and implement management's ideas.

4 | USING MODAL EXPRESSIONS OF NECESSITY

Read this advice column, in which "Dear Doctor" answers questions from readers.
Complete the column. Use the words or expressions in the box above each section.

~~am I supposed to~~	can	can't	should

Dear Doctor:

Where _____am I supposed to_____ find the time to exercise? I know I
        1.

_____can't_____ exercise, but I _____should_____ really fit it into my busy
    2.   **3.**

day. What's more, I hate jumping around and lifting weights and all that stuff. Is there

something I _____can_____ do instead of going to the gym?
        4.

Sincerely,

Discouraged

can	don't have to	must	ought	should	shouldn't

Dear Discouraged:

There's good news for you! You _____don't have to_____ do all those activities that are
        5.

so unpleasant for you. Instead, you _____can_____ get many of the same health
        6.

benefits just by being more active in your daily routine. For example, instead of parking

near the supermarket or the front door of an office building, you _____should_____
        7.

choose a spot at the far end of the parking lot.

In addition, you _____should not_____ take the elevator to go up a few floors. Say to
        8.

yourself: "It's good for my health and necessary to be more active. I definitely will not take

the elevator! I _____must_____ walk up instead." Similarly, in place of using
        9.

public transportation or driving, you _____ought_____ to walk to as many places as
        10.

you can.

can	don't have to	must

Taking just these few suggestions will give you quite a bit of extra activity. Recent research has shown that by taking this more active approach to daily living, you ___*can*___ avoid weight gain even if you consume the same number of
11.
calories. If you use up only 100 fewer calories per day and eat the same amount as usual, you will gain 10 pounds a year. So you ___*don't have to*___ be on a strict diet, but you
12.
___*must.*___ be active. Being active is the key; it is absolutely essential.
13.

had better not	might OR could	must	ought	should	shouldn't

Here are some important suggestions for adding activity to your daily life: At the office, you ___*should*___ walk over to your colleague's office to discuss something
14.
instead of e-mailing him. You ___*shouldn't*___ drive a half-mile to have lunch at
15.
a restaurant—walk there and back instead! And, if you live within 5 miles of work, you
_____ to try bicycling instead of driving or taking the bus—you'll get to
16.
like it, I promise.

Try these possibilities as well: At home and on weekends, you _____
17.
garden, wash your car, polish furniture, rake leaves, or even sweep or mop the floor.

Here's a rule to live by, and you ___*must*___ always keep this in mind
18.
wherever you are: I ___*had better not*___ let the fat creep up on me!
19.
Yours in good health,

Harry Healthmore, M.D.

5 | USING MODAL EXPRESSIONS OF NECESSITY

When you are invited to someone's home for dinner, do you take a gift? If so, what kind of gift is appropriate? Read this story of a Japanese student who faced this dilemma when he was in the United States. Complete the story. Use the modal expressions in the box.

are supposed to say	could find
could have been	could have brought
could have learned	didn't have to bring
had better be	have to pay
~~must take~~	should have brought
should I buy	should I have bought
was supposed to do	will have to come

WHAT'S THE RIGHT THING TO DO?

Tetsuya is a Japanese student who has been studying English in the United States for about six months. Last Saturday he went to the home of one of his American friends, Jason, who had invited Tetsuya to have dinner with him and his family.

Since this was Tetsuya's first dinner with an American family, he was a little nervous. He thought to himself, "As a guest, I ____*must take*____ a gift to the family, as we do in Japan." "What ____*what should I buy*____?" he wondered. He decided to buy a watermelon, which is a very desirable and prestigious gift in Japan.

He chose the most delicious-looking watermelon that he ____*could find*____. To Tetsuya, American watermelons seemed big—much bigger than Japanese watermelons, which are round, not long and oval as they are in the United States. In Japan, watermelons are quite expensive; you ____*have to*____ $15 to $20 for a nice one.

He took his watermelon home and placed it in a nice box, which he then wrapped with pretty paper. He left his apartment at 6:30, carrying his heavy gift. As he walked to Jason's house and his arm began to hurt, he began to wonder about the watermelon. "____*Should I have bought*____ the watermelon?" he thought to himself.

Tetsuya arrived at Jason's house at 7:00 sharp. Jason had told him, "My mom is a very punctual person who doesn't like late people, so you ____*had better be*____ on time at

7:00, or she'll get angry!" Of course, Jason was just joking, but he wanted Tetsuya to arrive as close to 7:00 as possible.

When Tetsuya arrived at Jason's home, he was welcomed graciously, and he gave the beautifully wrapped watermelon to Jason's mother. Jason's mother opened the box and said, "Oh, isn't this—um—interesting . . . a watermelon. What a nice gift! Well, Tetsuya! You _didn't have to bring_ anything, but we do thank you very much for your gift."
7.

Actually, she didn't know what she _was supposed to_ with the watermelon. She
8.
had already prepared a lovely dessert, and besides, there was no time to chill the watermelon.

Tetsuya quickly replied, "It's just a small uninteresting gift," which is a translation of a Japanese expression that you _are supposed to say_ whenever you give a gift to someone.
9.

Jason's mother smiled at Tetsuya and put the watermelon in the kitchen. "We'll enjoy this tomorrow," she said politely. "You _will have to come_ back to eat it with us then."
10.

Tetsuya then realized that the watermelon was not a very good gift idea because watermelons are not considered special in the United States. He still didn't know, however, what sort of gift he _should have bought_ instead. But, it really didn't matter. The evening was a great
11.
success. Jason's family was very welcoming, and Tetsuya appreciated their hospitality. Perhaps Tetsuya _could have bought_ something else, and perhaps Jason's family
12.
could have learned more about Japanese customs beforehand, but the warmth
13.
and good feelings that were exchanged were more valuable than any material gift
could have been .
14.

6 | EDITING

*Read this story by an English teacher. If the underlined phrase is wrong, write the correction above it. If it is correct, write **C** above it.*

        can

This is a true story about one of my students, Ana. I <u>can to</u> remember the first day she came

    C

to my class: She <u>couldn't</u> speak any English at all. She spoke only Spanish.

One time during the holidays between school terms, the dorms were closed, so the students

had to find

<u>have to find</u> a place to live during the break. Ana stayed with an American host family, and after

the vacation, she asked me what she <u>might ~~to~~ do</u> to thank her new friends for their hospitality.

     C   *might*

"Well, you <u>could send</u> them a gift," I told her. "Or you <u>must just send</u> them a nice card."

       would

Ana decided that she <u>~~will~~ send</u> a card. She asked, "<u>Am I supposed to get</u> a separate card for

each member of the family?"

      don't have to do   *C*

"No, you <u>haven't to do</u> that. What you <u>ought to do</u> is get a nice card for the family and write

a thoughtful message inside."

"But my English is not so good," she protested.

"OK, bring me the card, and I'll help you write your message," I offered.

                 C

Ana was extremely busy and easily <u>could have forgotten</u> her good intentions, but she didn't.

The next day after class, she showed me a beautiful card. On the front of it were the words "In

sympathy." On the inside were the words "You have my deepest sympathy. You are in my

thoughts at this time."

This was a big mistake! The card that Ana had bought was a sympathy card, a card that you

send when someone has died. Ana had confused the Spanish word "simpatico," which translates

to "nice" in English, with the English word "sympathy," which expresses the emotions of feeling

sorry about someone's death.

When Ana realized her mistake, she had a good, long laugh. She said that she <u>must have asked</u>

                                     does not need

someone to help her pick out the right card. Now Ana's English is excellent, and she <u>must not need</u>

any help any more.

7 | **PERSONALIZATION**

   Life presents us with many opportunities to do different things. Sometimes we take advantage of an opportunity—we choose to do something new or different. Sometimes we miss an opportunity—we don't do it. Think about a time when you had a chance to do something but you didn't do it. What was the opportunity? Why didn't you choose to do it? Are you happy or sad that you didn't? What did you learn from the experience?

Write two or three paragraphs about the opportunity that you missed. Use some of the phrases in the box.

I shouldn't have . . .
Instead, I should have . . .
I could/might have . . .
I didn't realize that I was supposed to . . .
Because of that missed opportunity, I had to . . .
In the future, I have to . . .
In the future, I should . . .
I have learned that I'd better . . .

_____

_____

_____

_____

_____

_____

_____

_____

_____

_____

_____

_____

_____

UNIT
6 Modals to Express Degrees of Certainty

1 | USING MODAL EXPRESSIONS OF CERTAINTY

Read these introductions to online news stories. What can you conclude about the missing information? Complete the sentences. Use the phrases in the box.

be in jail	be operating well	be very angry	be very effective
~~have been bad~~	have cheated	have snowed recently	have won a big victory
like skiing	speak Japanese	want to anger the voters	

Today's Top Stories

1. <u>Food Poisoning at Seafood Heaven</u>. Forty-six people who ate the shrimp at Seafood Heaven, a restaurant on the western shore, last Thursday night became ill with food poisoning. Other people who ate at the restaurant were unaffected.

   The shrimp must _____*have been bad*_____.

2. <u>34 Percent of Students Admit Cheating</u>. Thirty-four percent of college students admit they have cheated on tests or on written work during their academic career. An example of an otherwise honest person is Henry S., who . . .

   Henry S. must _____.

3. <u>Scam Impoverishes Senior Citizens</u>. Police in Minnesota arrested three con men for running an illegal operation that took hundreds of thousands of dollars from several elders in that state. In many cases, the money was the life savings of . . .

   These senior citizens must _____.

   The three con men now must _____.

4. <u>Hurricane Lashes Coast</u>. Winds of 120 miles per hour and tides as high as 10 feet whipped the shores of North Carolina early this morning. We cannot confirm the reports, but it is believed . . .

   Communications in the storm area must not _____.

5. <u>Heavy Response to Request to House International Tennis Players</u>. Sixteen students from various countries arrived in Springfield today for the annual College Tennis Championships. A call had gone out especially for hosts who can speak Japanese, and eight households responded with offers of hospitality for . . .

   The people in these households must _____.

6. <u>New Anti-Headache Medicine</u>. A new medication used to treat severe and frequent headaches has relieved symptoms dramatically in 86 percent of patients . . .

   The new medication must _____.

7. <u>Congress at a Standstill</u>. A proposal to enact new legislation to raise income taxes has not gone very far in the House of Representatives. Although everyone agrees that more money is necessary to run government programs, very few legislators want to go on record as supporting higher taxes . . .

   The legislators must not _____.

8. <u>Pennsylvania Players Celebrate in Philadelphia</u>. The Pennsylvania Men's Soccer Team came home to a wild celebration in downtown Philadelphia yesterday. Pictured are . . .

   The soccer team from Pennsylvania must _____.

9. <u>Unseasonable Heat in Europe</u>. An unseasonable heat wave lingers in Switzerland, Italy, Austria, and France, causing the cancellation of thousands of bookings for the Christmas ski season and . . .

   It must not _____.

   The people who canceled must _____.

2 | USING MODAL EXPRESSIONS OF CERTAINTY

Circle the correct modal auxiliaries to complete the hints below these trivia items. Then circle the letter of the correct answer.

INTERESTING WORLD FACTS

1. The longest river in the world is . . .

HINT: The river is in Africa, so it <u>might</u> / (<u>has to</u>) be the Nile.

(**a.**) the Nile.　　　**b.** the Mississippi.　　**c.** the Danube.

2. The highest waterfalls in the world are . . .

HINT: The falls are in South America, so the answer <u>must not</u> / <u>can't</u> be Niagara Falls or Victoria Falls.

a. Niagara Falls.　　**b.** Victoria Falls.　　**c.** Angel Falls.

3. The highest mountain in the world is Mt. Everest. It's located in . . .

HINT: Turkey does not have extremely high mountains, so the answer <u>might</u> / <u>must</u> be India, or it <u>could</u> / <u>must</u> be Nepal and Tibet.

a. India.　　　**b.** Turkey.　　**c.** Nepal and Tibet.

4. The country with the longest coastline in the world is . . .

HINT: The country is in the Western Hemisphere, so it <u>might</u> / <u>must</u> be Canada.

a. Australia.　　**b.** Canada.　　**c.** the Philippines.

5. The country with the largest land area is . . .

HINT: The country has, mostly, a cold climate, and it is in the Northern Hemisphere. It <u>could</u> / <u>should</u> be Russia, or it <u>could</u> / <u>should</u> be Canada.

a. Russia.　　**b.** Canada.　　**c.** Brazil.

6. Early in the 21st century, the country with the largest population was . . .

HINT: This country's capital is Beijing. According to projections, in 2028 this country <u>must</u> / <u>should</u> no longer have the largest population in the world because of its strong efforts to limit the size of its families.

a. China.　　**b.** India.　　**c.** the United States of America.

7. This country has played in the most final contests of the World Cup: . . .

HINT: The people in this country don't speak Spanish, so it <u>might</u> / <u>should</u> be Brazil, or it <u>might</u> / <u>should</u> be Italy.

a. Brazil.　　**b.** Argentina.　　**c.** Italy.

8. The country where they drink the most coffee per person is . . .

   HINT: In this country, they <u>can / must</u> drink a lot of coffee—1,581 cups per year per person—in order to keep warm!

   a. Guatemala.   **b.** Finland.   **c.** Egypt.

3 | USING MODAL EXPRESSIONS OF CERTAINTY

Two teachers in an English language program are talking about their students. Complete the teachers' statements. Circle the correct modals. You will have to use the information in the chart to complete some of the statements.

NUMBER OF CLASSES IN THE PROGRAM			
Beginning–1	Intermediate–2	Advanced–6	
STUDENT NAME	**COUNTRY**	**CLASS**	**EMPLOYMENT GOAL**
Beyhan Nurev	**Turkey**	**Intermediate**	**to be an accountant**
Hiba Rashid	**Jordan**	**Beginning**	**to work in an international bank**
Jared Larson	**Sweden**	**Beginning**	**to be a chemical engineer**
Jenny Chan	**Singapore**	**Advanced**	**to teach English in Singapore**
Mario Rivas	**Mexico**	**Intermediate**	**to be a computer engineer**
Roberto Beltran	**Colombia**	**Advanced**	**to work in public relations**

1. Some of the students have cars. Beyhan <u>must /</u>(might) have a car, but I'm not sure.

2. Mario <u>might / must</u> speak English better than Jared.

3. Jenny <u>might / must</u> be older than Hiba.

4. Jared <u>might / must</u> know who Hiba is.

5. Roberto <u>could / couldn't</u> know Mario.

6. Jenny speaks English and Chinese. Hiba speaks Arabic and English. They had lunch together yesterday. They <u>could / must</u> have spoken to each other in English.

7. Mario <u>may / must</u> have traveled to France and England.

8. Jenny is only 18 years old. She <u>must / could</u> not have taught English in a high school.

9. Mario <u>must / might not</u> know something about computers already.

10. Beyhan <u>might / must</u> be interested in numbers.

11. Jared <u>might / must</u> have seen snow.

(continued)

12. Mario isn't very happy at this school. He thinks that it <u>might / might not</u> have been a mistake to attend this college.

13. Jenny and Roberto are both advanced students, but they <u>may / may not</u> be in the same class.

14. Hiba and Roberto <u>can't / might not</u> be in the same class.

15. Beyhan failed the last test, but all of the other students passed it. Beyhan admits that the test was actually quite easy. She <u>must / must not</u> have studied very much.

16. Jared is really interested in chemistry. Both his parents are chemists. He is a hard worker. He <u>should / must</u> be very successful in this field in the future.

4 | USING MODAL EXPRESSIONS OF CERTAINTY

Read these excerpts from different conversations heard in the halls of a high school. Circle the letter of the modal expression that completes each statement correctly.

1. **A:** I need an easy math class. Which teacher's class is easy?

   B: Take Mr. Pembroke's class. It _____ be very easy. He usually teaches children.

   a. may   **b.** could   **c.** should

2. **A:** Do you know where I can find some aspirin?

   B: The office _____ it. They have everything.

   a. ought to have had   **b.** must have   **c.** must have had

3. **A:** How old is Mr. McKenna?

   B: Oh, he _____ over 50. He's been teaching here for 30 years!

   a. 's got to be   **b.** could be   **c.** might be

4. **A:** Juan said he missed 12 questions on the test.

   B: He _____ missed 12 questions! The test had only 10 questions.

   a. couldn't have   **b.** might not have   **c.** must not have

5. **A:** I've been looking for Ms. Cloves. Isn't her office in Room 212?

   B: I thought so, but she _____.

   a. may have moved   **b.** had to have moved   **c.** could move

6. **A:** Where's Ms. Fowler? She's not in her office!

   B: She _____ in class or she _____ at a meeting.

      a. might be; might be   **b.** must be; must be   **c.** should be; should be

7. **A:** Where's Mr. Lamar? It's 11:00 and he's not here yet.

   B: He _____ be here soon. He's never more than 5 minutes late.

      a. must   **b.** could   **c.** ought to

8. **A:** Franco looks really sad today. What do you think happened?

   B: He _____ passed his chemistry exam. He was really worried about it.

      a. couldn't have   **b.** must not have   **c.** can't have

9. **A:** I hear that school's going to be closed for a holiday tomorrow. It's the principal's birthday.

   B: That _____ be true! School is never closed for a reason like that!

      a. may not   **b.** might not   **c.** can't

10. **A:** Do you know where Ms. Banta is? She's not in her office.

    B: She _____ home sick. I know she wasn't feeling well this morning.

      a. must have gone   **b.** has to go   **c.** ought to go

5 | USING MODAL EXPRESSIONS

Three friends have just arrived at a restaurant, and they are talking about their choices.
Complete their pre-dinner conversation. Use the modals and verbs in the box.

can still do	could have eaten	could have ordered
couldn't eat	might make	must be (3 times)
~~must have~~	ought to be / should be (2 times)	should take

NANCY: I wonder if they serve cheeseburgers here. I don't see it on the menu.

  BILL: I saw a poster with all sorts of sandwiches on it by the door, so I'm sure they

   _____ *must have* _____ cheeseburgers. Keep looking. It
                  1.

   _____ on the menu somewhere.
             2.

SHARON: Wow, listen to this. They have a sandwich that has roast chicken, roast beef, and

   cheese. It's covered with a special mayonnaise sauce. Doesn't that sound great?

(continued)

BILL: Are you kidding? I _____ that. Do you know how unhealthy

that sandwich is? Do you realize how fattening that _____?
4.

SHARON: Well, I don't care. It _____ me fat, but it won't kill me. And it
5.

sounds delicious. Nancy, what are you going to have?

NANCY: Well, I'm not that hungry, so I'm looking for something that's not too filling. What

about this vegetable snack plate?

BILL: Hmmm . . . yes, that _____ light. Why don't you get that?
6.

NANCY: I've never ordered that here before. It sounds like it _____
7.

perfect.

BILL: I feel like eating barbecue, but they don't have that here.

SHARON: We drove past Bob's Barbecue when we came here. We _____
8.

there. You should have said something!

BILL: You're right. I forgot about that place. Let's go there.

NANCY: When? You mean now?

BILL: Yeah, sure. We haven't ordered yet, so we _____ that.
9.

NANCY: You _____ crazy! I'm not getting up and leaving a restaurant.
10.

How embarrassing!

SHARON: It's too late, because here comes the waitress.

WAITRESS: Hi, are you folks ready to order?

NANCY: I'll have the vegetable snack plate. And I'd like iced tea, please.

SHARON: I'd like the beef, chicken, and cheese sandwich, please. And bring me iced tea as well.

BILL: I'll have a roast chicken sandwich and iced tea to drink.

WAITRESS: OK, we're not too busy right now, so your orders _____ only
11.

about 10 minutes. I'll be right back with your drinks.

(*The waitress leaves.*)

SHARON: Hey, Bill, look at that sign. It says they have a barbecued beef sandwich.

BILL: Oh, no. I didn't see it! So I _____ barbecue after all.
12.

6 | USING MODAL EXPRESSIONS OF CERTAINTY

Read this information about a crime. Write whether the sentences below it are **True** *or* **False**. *Then write short explanations for your answers.*

There was a murder at the Nelsons' house last night. Mr. Nelson, a very wealthy 80-year-old man, was murdered. The police are investigating, and they believe someone in the house was the murderer. The murder happened at about 10 P.M. The police found the body in the living room. The police are sure only one person committed this crime.

PERSONS IN THE NELSONS' HOUSE

Mildred	wife	She is old and walks with a cane. She was asleep by 9:30 P.M.
Belinda	cousin	She is 35 years old. She was envious of the Nelson's wealth.
Mark	cousin	He is Belinda's husband. He didn't come home until 11 P.M.
Georgia	cousin	She is Belinda and Mark's baby. She is only 6 months old.
Frank	brother	Frank is visiting from New York. He loved his brother very much and is sincerely upset over this matter.
Karla	the maid	Karla has been with the Nelsons for over 30 years. She usually goes to bed at 10 P.M., but last night she was awake in her room until midnight.

_____*True*_____ **1.** Karla could have heard the murder.

   *It's possible. She was awake at the time.*_____

_____ **2.** Georgia could have killed Mr. Nelson.

   _____

   _____

_____ **3.** The murderer might have used poison to kill Mr. Nelson.

   _____

   _____

_____ **4.** Belinda might have killed Mr. Nelson.

   _____

   _____

_____ **5.** Mildred must have killed her husband.

   _____

   _____

(continued)

UNIT

7 Count and Non-Count Nouns

1 | IDENTIFYING COUNT AND NON-COUNT NOUNS

Read this passage. If the underlined word is a count noun, write **C** *above it. If it is a non-count noun, write* **NC**.

                                              NC

        Why does <u>communication</u> provide such a fascinating <u>object</u> of <u>study</u>? Perhaps because of its unique role in capturing the <u>breadth</u> of human <u>thought</u> and <u>endeavor</u>. We look around us and are awed by the variety of several thousand <u>languages</u> and <u>dialects</u> expressing a multiplicity of worldviews, literatures, and ways of <u>life</u>. We look back at the <u>thoughts</u> of our predecessors, and find we can see only as far as <u>language</u> lets us see.

        We look forward in <u>time</u>, and find we can plan only through language. We look outward in <u>space</u>, and send <u>symbols</u> of <u>communication</u> along with our spacecraft, to explain who we are, in case there is anyone out there who wants to know.

2 | RECOGNIZING NON-COUNT NOUNS

Read this article about Vancouver. There are 29 non-count nouns. The first one is underlined. Find and underline 28 more.

What does it take for a city to be voted the "Best City in the Americas"? It takes top scores in a poll that includes <u>ambience</u>, friendliness, culture, restaurants, lodging, and shopping. This year the city that ranked highest in all areas was Vancouver, British Columbia.

Located on the west coast of Canada, Vancouver has a wonderful climate, with mild weather and clean air. Although it is far north—at latitude 49°16'N—the winters are not cold because of the warm Pacific currents that flow by. Wherever you look in the area, you see spectacular scenery: The city is surrounded by mountains capped with snow, and you are never far from the sea.

The water and the nearby wilderness provide plenty of opportunities for outdoor recreation: hiking, camping, skiing, and all watersports. Because of the attributes of nature, the area attracts outdoor enthusiasts, and tourism is important here.

In addition, Vancouver has a large number of cultural events, especially in the fields of music, art, and dance. There is plenty of entertainment—theaters, concerts, art shows, and festivals—as well as many fine shops and restaurants.

The economy is usually strong. Vancouver is a major port, and it offers easy transportation to all parts of Canada. Because of its ideal location and multicultural community, Vancouver is the gateway of commerce to the entire Pacific Rim. Downtown Vancouver is the headquarters for many businesses in the fields of forestry and mining, as well as in software, biotechnology, and most recently, movies.

If Vancouver sounds like the perfect city for livability, to many of its residents it is. They take pride in their city. They expect thousands of visitors in 2010, when Vancouver will host the Winter Olympics.

3 | MATCHING PHRASES WITH NON-COUNT NOUNS

Match the non-count nouns on the left with the correct phrases of measurement on the right.

__*j*__ **1.** equipment

_____ **2.** electricity

_____ **3.** French bread

_____ **4.** gasoline

_____ **5.** iced tea with lemon

_____ **6.** news

_____ **7.** rain

_____ **8.** brown rice

_____ **9.** science

_____ **10.** tennis

a. a bolt of

b. a different branch of

c. a few drops of

d. 12 gallons of

e. a nice game of

f. three glasses of

g. a grain of

h. an interesting item of

i. two loaves of

j. ~~a heavy piece of~~

4 | USING PHRASES WITH NON-COUNT NOUNS

Read this letter. Complete the letter with the phrases in the box. Some phrases will be used more than once, and in some places more than one phrase is appropriate.

a bit of	a clap of	a flash of
a game of	a glass of	a period of
a piece of	a serving of	a slice of

Dear Mary,

You know how much I dislike picnics. Ted insisted that we go on one before the summer ended, and although I resisted, I am so glad that we finally did that. First, he did all the work. He wouldn't let me do any work. Of course, he wouldn't accept _____a piece of_____ advice
1.
from me, either.

We drove off on Saturday morning to Grover's Cove, which is a pleasant, secluded area where we met three other couples. At first the weather was fine. We decided to have
_____ volleyball before lunch. But our friends had forgotten the net, so we
2.
forgot about the volleyball game and sat down to play _____ cards and
3.
drink _____ lemonade.
4.

At lunch, as usual, I ate too much. I had _____ Sheila's special seven-
5.
grain bread, _____ Ted's delicious curried chicken salad,
6.
_____ Saga bleu cheese, _____ Sheila's famous
7. **8.**
apple pie, and _____ cranberry juice. We settled in to listen to
9.
_____ music by Mozart, the Violin Concerto 3, on the portable CD player.
10.

Just as we were dozing off comfortably on our blankets, we heard _____
11.
thunder, which really startled us. Then we saw _____ lightning nearby, so we
12.
packed up hurriedly and got into our cars. When we turned on the car radio, we heard
_____ news: Tornadoes were in the area, and it was going to be dangerous
13.
to be outside for _____ time.
14.

We were quite anxious, but we made it home safely and stayed together singing old songs for the rest of the afternoon. We really had a wonderful day. I'm sorry you weren't with us.

Your friend,

LeAnn

5 | USING COUNT AND NON-COUNT NOUNS

Read this passage reporting the results of a survey that asked people what they valued most in life. Complete the passage. Circle the correct count or non-count forms.

SURVEY RESULTS

As expected, (good health)/ a good health was cited as the number one factor necessary to have
1.
a happy life.

Having <u>partner / a partner</u> to share the ups and downs of life was the next most important
2.
factor. In describing what they valued or would value in the partner, people said they wanted to
spend their lives with someone who had <u>integrity / an integrity</u>, who wasn't afraid of <u>work / a</u>
3.   **4.**
<u>work</u> but at the same time was capable of having <u>great fun / a great fun</u>, and who would give
5.
<u>love / a love</u> generously. Interestingly, more men than women mentioned that they wanted their
6.
partners to be intelligent. Women tended to mention <u>practicality / a practicality</u> as a feature they
7.
desired in a relationship.

The third factor following <u>a compatible companion / compatible companion</u> in importance
8.
was a strong family, cited equally by both sexes. Evidently, people yearn for connections and
<u>warmth / a warmth</u>.
9.

Also high on the list was having <u>career / a career</u> that is fulfilling, and <u>job / a job</u> that provides
10.   **11.**
satisfaction. <u>Good salary / A good salary</u> was not the only consideration; most people said that
12.
they also wanted to receive <u>respect / a respect</u> for their work.
13.

6 | USING COUNT AND NON-COUNT NOUNS

A *Quickly read this menu, which includes many foods that originated with the Native American peoples. Some of these foods are described in the sentences on the following page.*

Mitsitam Native Foods Café
National Museum of the American Indian, Washington, D.C.

Authentic Soups and Chowders, made from

Peanuts	Cup $2.95	Bowl $4.95
Pumpkin	Cup $2.95	Bowl $4.95
Quahog Clams	Cup $3.95	Bowl $5.95
Black Beans	Cup $2.95	Bowl $4.95

Salads, made of

Wild Rice and Watercress	$2.95
Jicama, Black Beans, and Tomatoes	$2.95

Main Dishes

Maple Roasted Turkey	$6.95, with 2 sides $ 9.95
Cedar Planked Fire-Roasted	
Juniper Salmon	$7.95, with 2 sides $10.95

Sides

Ash Roasted Sweet Corn on the Cob	$2.95
Succotash, made of Beans and Corn	$2.95
Molasses Baked Beans	$2.95
Honey Baked Golden Beets	$2.95
Refried Pinto Beans	$2.95

Sweets

Indian Pudding	$3.50
Tasty Tart, made with	
Cranberries and Apples	$3.50
Watermelon Agua Fresca	$2.50

B *Complete the sentences. Use the nouns in the box. Add the indefinite article **a** or a plural ending when necessary. Some nouns are used more than once in an item.*

bean	~~corn~~	cranberry
peanut	pumpkin	salmon
tomato	turkey	wild rice

1. This golden vegetable has been basic to Native American cooking since about 6000 B.C. It is used to make tortillas, among other things. It's _____ *corn* _____.

2. Popular in jellies and winter desserts, these red berries are also used to make a healthful juice. They're _____.

3. This vegetable comes in many varieties and colors. It is high in carbohydrates, and it forms the basis of many Central American and Caribbean dishes. We buy this product today in cans or in packages. It's _____.

4. This vegetable is large, round, and orange. It is used in soup, breads, and pies. When referring to one, we call it _____. When used in cooking, it is called _____.

5. This large bird is now part of the American Thanksgiving holiday. One of them is called _____. As a main course, it is called _____.

6. This pink-fleshed fish thrives in cold water. When you catch one, you catch _____. As a main course, it is called _____.

7. Round and red, these are used in salads and as the basis of many pasta sauces. They're _____.

8. This grain grows in moist places all over the world. It can be served with meat, vegetables, and even fruit. The Native Americans grow a special kind. It's called _____.

9. Originating in Brazil and Peru, we now use these as a snack and in candy. They are also used as the basis of many sauces in Southeast Asia. They're _____.

7 | EDITING

Read this passage about communication. There are 17 mistakes in the use of count and non-count nouns. The first mistake is already corrected. Find and correct 16 more.

Spoken language is $\overset{a}{\wedge}$ fascinating thing, enabling us to communicate feelings and thoughts, to tell stories, and even to tell lie. Early in the history of a humankind, the use of symbols to transmit idea took communication one step further. It was not necessary to be in the actual sight of another human being when one could send signals by smokes or drums. But, how could this communications be kept in any permanent form?

People began to record markings on hard surfaces like clays, using symbols to represent peoples, animals, or, later, various abstraction. Over many thousands of years, the pictures developed into many different alphabet.

What would the world be like without writing and reading? How would knowledges pass from one generation to another? Though they are necessary today, writing and reading were not always two skill to be taken for granted. In fact, until recent years, a literacy has not been as widespread as it is now.

Technology is advancing the ways that informations is sent and received. Computer literacy have been added to reading and writing as a basic and necessary capability. Today, person is able to learn anything from any part of the world, and to easily communicate with anyone on any part of globe. We have come a long way from smoke signals in the universal instinct to connect.

8 | PERSONALIZATION

People differ greatly in their likes and dislikes. How would you describe yours? Write two or three paragraphs describing the things you like and dislike. Use some of the phrases in the box.

My favorite place is . . .	In school, my favorite subjects are/were . . .
Some of my favorite foods are . . .	In school, my least favorite subjects are/were . . .
My favorite beverages are . . .	Two sports that I like are . . .
Some of the activities I like most are . . .	Two careers that interest me are . . .
Activities I dislike include . . .	For me, the best things in life are . . .

_____

_____

_____

_____

_____

_____

_____

_____

_____

_____

_____

_____

_____

_____

_____

_____

_____

_____

8 Definite and Indefinite Articles

1 | USING ARTICLES

Read the text of an e-mail in which Sara describes a family reunion to her cousin Elaine.
Complete the e-mail. Circle the correct articles, or — if no article is needed.

Dear Elaine:

Sorry you missed the family reunion last weekend! I'll try to bring you up to date:

First, Uncle Jasper is now the /ⓐ professor at a / — small college in Wyoming. He teaches the / —
                              1.   **2.**   **3.**
philosophy. He loves living out there. He lives on a / — ranch with his wife, who is — / a
                                                    4.   **5.**
psychiatrist, and his son, who is the / a student. A / The ranch is not big, and they raise cattle.
                                     6.   **7.**

Then, there is our cousin Melissa. She just retired. She doesn't have to worry about a / —
                                                                                        8.
money because she had been saving all her life, and now she is traveling all over — / the world.
                                                                                  9.
You should hear a / the stories she tells about her travels!
              10.

Cousin Bert is looking for the / a job, again. Poor Bert! He liked the / a good job he had at the
                            11.   **12.**
software company, but unfortunately, it went out of business last year. He's a / — really sweet guy.
                                                                             13.
It's the / a pity that he's always out of a / — work.
     14.   **15.**

Bob and Betty have seven grandchildren now. Their daughter Karen just had the / — twin
                                                                            16.
boys! Bob is never going to retire. He likes practicing a / — law, and he loves being the / a lawyer.
                                                       17.   **18.**
Betty continues doing a / — volunteer work at the hospital and at the museum.
                      19.

Cousin Jennifer is a / — producer for — / a comedy show on the / — TV. I don't remember
                   20.   **21.**   **22.**
the / a network it is on, but it is a / — very popular show. She was at a / the reunion with a / the
23.   **24.**   **25.**   **26.**
really nice guy, and she's going to marry him! A / The wedding is going to be in June.
                                            27.

You'll be at the / a next reunion, I hope. It's going to be in two years.
              28.

—Sara

2 | USING ARTICLES

Read these job ads from an environmental jobs page on the Internet. Complete the ads.
Circle the correct articles, or — if no article is needed.

ENVIRONMENTAL JOBS

Associate Zoological Veterinarian

Requires a degree in <u>a</u> / <u>⊖</u> veterinary medicine from <u>a / the</u> recognized university, and

1.   **2.**

two to three years of <u>an / —</u> experience in <u>a / the</u> medical care of wild animals in a

                 3.   **4.**

zoological institute. Extensive knowledge of <u>the / —</u> wildlife and <u>a / —</u> wildlife

                                     5.   **6.**

behavior is highly desirable. <u>The / A</u> salary is above average. Excellent benefits.

                               7.

Coordinator of Endangered Species

This is <u>— / a</u> unique opportunity for <u>an / —</u> experienced and highly motivated

         8.   **9.**

professional to deal with issues regarding endangered species. Three years in <u>a / the</u>

                                                                     10.

program or institute protecting endangered species is necessary, and one year at a

technical or professional level in <u>the / —</u> researching and analyzing data. A Master's

                                   11.

degree or higher is desirable. Salary: $4,016 per month, plus generous benefits.

Fisheries Biologist

Our small commercial company needs <u>a / the</u> field biologist to test fish on commercial

                                          12.

fishing boats off <u>a / the</u> coast of Alaska. <u>A / The</u> position requires a Master's degree in

              13.   **14.**

<u>— / the</u> biology or other natural science, <u>a / —</u> college-level statistics course, and <u>the / a</u>

15.   **16.**   **17.**

flexible attitude. Applicants can expect strenuous working conditions, but <u>a / the</u> good

                                                                 18.

salary commensurate with their experience. Apply to <u>a / the</u> head office in Juneau.

                                             19.

Environmental Microbiology

<u>A / The</u> Department of <u>the / —</u> Civil Engineering at <u>the / —</u> University of Atlantis invites

20.   **21.**   **22.**

<u>the / —</u> applications for <u>an / —</u> associate professor position. We are particularly

23.   **24.**

interested in candidates with <u>an / —</u> extensive experience in <u>the / —</u> research. The

                               25.   **26.**

successful candidate will demonstrate a background of high-quality teaching at the

undergraduate and graduate levels, and must have a Ph.D. <u>The / A</u> highest possible

                                                                      27.

salary is offered.

3 | USING ARTICLES

Read the text of an e-mail from Marco to Ricardo. Complete the e-mail. Circle the correct articles, or — if no article is needed.

Dear Ricardo,

Things have gotten better since I last wrote to you. First, I received ⓐ / — letter from my
1.
family with the / a very nice surprise in it: the / a check for $200. A / The letter made me feel
2.   **3.**   **4.**
good because I thought my family had forgotten me, and the / — check made me feel even better.
5.
With the / a money, I went to an / — expensive restaurant downtown with a / — new friend.
6.   **7.**   **8.**
Yes, the / a new friend is the / a beautiful young woman. If our relationship develops, I'll tell you
9.   **10.**
her name in the / a next letter I write to you. What I will tell you for now is that she is the / —
11.   **12.**
only daughter of the / an president of my university.
13.

By the way, the / — weather has improved, too. We haven't had the / — rain for three weeks
14.   **15.**
now. I've seen the / a sun every day, and last weekend I went to the / — beach and got a / —
16.   **17.**   **18.**
bad sunburn.

Do you know anything about the / — American football? It's a / — really rough game played
19.   **20.**
by two teams with 11 people on each team. The / A team that has the / — ball is supposed to
21.   **22.**
take it into an / the opposing team's territory and score a touchdown—it's like a goal in our
23.
football—and that means they get six points. At first, I didn't understand it, but I've gone to a
few games and I see that it's exciting but more dangerous than a / the game we play at home.
24.
Here they call our game the / — soccer.
25.

My classes are going better, too. I like the / — organic chemistry and computer science. I even
26.
like the / — history now; the / a history course that I am taking focuses on the / — most
27.   **28.**   **29.**
important events of the 20th century. I like the / — English, even though I am just not very good
30.
in the / — languages.
31.

Well, Ricardo, I gotta go! That's the / — American English way of saying "I have got to go."
32.
Write me soon, OK?

—Marco

4 | USING ARTICLES

*Read this archaeologist's description of an abandoned city on the planet Green. Complete the description. Write the articles **a**, **an**, or **the** where appropriate. Write — if no article is needed.*

SITE: Planet Green

YEAR: A.D. 3005

NOTES: Abandoned City

Remains were found of what appears to be _____*a*_____ large city on _____ island in
                                          1.   **2.**
_____ Northern Hemisphere. It seems that _____ city was part of _____ advanced
3.   **4.**   **5.**
civilization.

What we had thought was _____ sophisticated canal system has turned out to be
                        6.
something else entirely. _____ canals that we thought we saw contained no water but were
                         7.
covered with _____ hard surface. We think these were actually _____ roadways that
             8.   **9.**
_____ vehicles traveled on. _____ vehicles had four wheels, and _____ pieces from
10.   **11.**   **12.**
thousands of them were seen.

_____ shadows that we had previously seen by telescope were actually _____ very
13.   **14.**
tall buildings, which _____ population probably lived in.
                      15.

We found no agricultural areas, although we did find _____ large open space in
                                                      16.
_____ middle of _____ island. Perhaps it was used as _____ large park.
17.   **18.**   **19.**

We are not sure how the inhabitants obtained their food; probably they brought it by boat

from _____ mainland, or over _____ bridge. We also found _____ parallel rows of
     20.   **21.**   **22.**
_____ iron, perhaps used for some form of _____ transportation. We suspect that the
23.   **24.**
inhabitants traveled by air, too, but we didn't find _____ evidence of any type of airport or air
                                                      25.
transportation vehicles.

We are not sure why _____ area was abandoned, but maybe it was because _____
                    26.   **27.**
entire planet was suffering from _____ severe pollution.
                                 28.

5 | USING THE DEFINITE ARTICLE OR NO ARTICLE WITH PLACE NAMES

*Read this letter from a travel agent to her client. Complete the letter. Write **the** where the definite article is needed. Write — if no definite article is needed.*

GLOBE TRAVEL

Dear Dorothea:

You will leave _____—_____ Los Angeles at 11 P.M. You'll be flying at night, so you
        1.

won't see _____ Rocky Mountains or _____ Mississippi River, which is
     2.   **3.**

really a pity.

After you leave _____ United States, you'll be flying off the coast of
         4.

_____ Canada, then over _____ Atlantic to _____ United
 5.   **6.**   **7.**

Kingdom. As you fly over _____ Europe, you will be able to see _____
                  8.   **9.**

France as you cross _____ Alps into _____ Switzerland. You'll land in
           10.   **11.**

_____ Geneva. You have reservations at _____ Sheraton Hotel where
 12.   **13.**

the conference is. I've reserved a place for you on the post-conference tour to _____
                                              14.

Hungary and _____ Czech Republic, so you'll be able to see a little of eastern
          15.

Europe. You'll be coming home on a different route, as you requested, so that you can stop in

_____ Florida to see your grandmother. It's too bad you won't be able to visit
 16.

_____ Haiti or _____ Dominican Republic or any other islands while
 17.   **18.**

you're in the area, as _____ Caribbean is a great place to relax after the hard work
                  19.

you will have been doing at the conference.

Your return flight is at 8 A.M. on Monday, the 15th, and you arrive home at 10:20 A.M.

Have a great trip!

Sincerely,

Ava Ray

Ava Ray, Travel Agent

6 | USING ARTICLES

*Read the following interview, in which Radio Station KESL (A) speaks with popular disc
jockey Nancy Stone (B). Complete the interview. Circle the correct articles, or — if no article
is needed.*

A: So, Nancy, why do you think <u>a / —</u> rock music is still so popular?
　　　　　　　　　　　　　　　　　　1.

B: Well, <u>the / —</u> rock music that I play on this station is classic and speaks to people everywhere.
　　　　2.

There are many variations of <u>a / —</u> rock, and I choose music that I know people will respond
　　　　　　　　　　　　　　　3.

to, <u>the / —</u> best songs, those that speak to <u>the / —</u> heart.
　　4.　　　　　　　　　　　　　　　**5.**

A: Do you mean songs about <u>the / —</u> love?
　　　　　　　　　　　　　6.

B: Yes, of course, but also songs about <u>a / —</u> pain and <u>a / —</u> longing.
　　　　　　　　　　　　　　　　7.　　　　　**8.**

A: Who are <u>the / a</u> most popular artists?
　　　　　　9.

B: My show plays mostly <u>a / —</u> light rock, you know, so we play a lot of the golden oldies, like
　　　　　　　　　　　10.

the Beatles, some Rolling Stones, even Elvis. Elton John remains <u>a / the</u> popular artist, maybe
　　　　　　　　　　　　　　　　　　　　　　　　　　11.

because of his association with <u>— / the</u> Princess Diana.
　　　　　　　　　　　　　　12.

A: What about <u>— / the</u> rap?
　　　　　　13.

B: Well, some people wonder whether or not it is really <u>a / —</u> music.
　　　　　　　　　　　　　　　　　　　　　14.

A: So do you play it?

B: Very little. A lot of our mature listeners don't like <u>the / —</u> lyrics and heavy beats of rap.
　　　　　　　　　　　　　　　　　　　15.

A: Any international songs?

B: Oh, yes, a lot. We play some songs of Julio Iglesias, the Scottish band Travis, or whoever is hot

at the time, and we often have requests for Brazilian music, for Caetano Veloso, for example.

This music is well known, and it's not necessary to speak <u>the / a</u> language in order to
　　　　　　　　　　　　　　　　　　　　　16.

appreciate it.

A: So <u>the / a</u> same music is appreciated all over the world?
　　　17.

B: It seems so. I've heard *I Want to Hold Your Hand* in elevators from <u>the / —</u> United States to
　　　　　　　　　　　　　　　　　　　　　　　　　　18.

<u>the / —</u> Europe to <u>the / —</u> Far East. I've heard *La Vie En Rose* on an airplane while flying
19.　　　　　　**20.**

(continued)

over the / — Andes Mountains and over the / — Atlantic, and even while flying over the / a
    21.   22.   23.

North Pole. Whether I stay in a / — Hilton Hotel in Chicago or one in Cairo, the / — music I
                       24.   25.

hear is the / — same. Culturally, you know, the / — planet is getting smaller and smaller.
     26.   27.

A: Yes, it's true. By the way, I've heard that some of the / — presidents of the United States have
                                             28.

been enthusiastic fans of pop music.

B: Of course! I think that both the Bush presidents were the / — country music fans. And Bill
                                               29.

Clinton liked a / the song *Chelsea Morning* so much that he named his daughter Chelsea.
         30.

A: What's your all-time favorite, Nancy?

B: Oh, I don't know, Bob. Actually, I'll tell you a / — secret: I really like the / — classical music
                                      31.   32.

most of all.

7 | EDITING

Read this flyer. There are 21 mistakes in the use of articles. The first mistake is already corrected. Find and correct 20 more, either by supplying correct articles or by omitting or replacing incorrect articles.

HELP THE METROPOLITAN ZOO!

     Your Metropolitan Zoo needs you! Can you adopt ^an animal? You can "adopt" an animal by contributing money for its care. By adopting an animal, you will help us keep zoo in good condition with the healthy animals, and you will have a satisfaction of knowing that your love and your efforts are keeping "your" animal alive and well.

Needing adoption right now are two tigers, one lion, two camels, a family of three chimpanzees, and one gorilla. Which animal would you like to adopt?

Here is some information about the animals needing adoption. Both our tigers are females; we are hoping to obtain male from Pakistan next year. A lion, recently named Mufasa by a group of the schoolchildren, is three years old. Both camels are Arabian kind, with one hump, not Bactrian kind, with two humps. Chimpanzees in our zoo act just like human family. They take care of each other, laugh, and sometimes even have the arguments. We have only one gorilla now; he is most popular animal at zoo, and also most expensive to maintain. He needs several sponsors. He puts on the show every afternoon by interacting with a visitors. He loves an applause that he gets.

After you adopt a animal, you will regularly be advised of its life situation. You will be honored at our annual spring banquet, and you will receive free admission to a zoo.

Please find it in your heart to contribute to well-being of our animals.

8 | PERSONALIZATION

Write a letter describing your hometown to someone who is about to visit there for the first time. Describe the character of your hometown and the most important places to see. Use some of the phrases in the box.

> When you come to my hometown, you will first notice the atmosphere of . . .
>
> The most prominent physical feature of my hometown is . . .
>
> The most prominent building in my hometown is . . .
>
> Some interesting things to see in my hometown include . . .
>
> Be sure to visit . . .
>
> In the evening, you can go to . . .
>
> The people are friendly and show a lot of . . .
>
> Near the center of town, you will find . . .
>
> My hometown is noted for . . .
>
> Although my hometown is new and modern, it doesn't have . . .
>
> Fortunately (Unfortunately), my hometown has (doesn't have) . . .
>
> I'm sure you will like . . .
>
> What I miss about my hometown is . . .

_____

_____

_____

_____

_____

_____

_____

_____

_____

_____

_____

Quantifiers

1 | RECOGNIZING QUANTIFIERS

Read this weather prediction for a year in the near future. There are 19 uses of quantifiers.
The first one is already underlined. Find and underline 18 more.

  THE INTERNATIONAL ALMANAC ONLINE

From November through March, <u>a lot of</u> warmer-than-usual weather is expected in much of the Northern Hemisphere, although not in every area. Certain parts of Europe—especially the British Isles and France—will be warm, but some parts of North America—notably western Canada and Alaska—will be somewhat colder. If the cold conditions in these two places combine with warm air currents from the coastal currents, there will be several heavy snowstorms in both areas. The northern parts of Asia will experience the usual cold winter with plenty of snow.

In western Africa, the weather will be cooler than usual, and may produce more rain. If there is enough precipitation in certain areas throughout the continent, crop production could be greater than usual. The river beds—a great many of which had dried up during the recent drought—will return to their normal state.

In the Southern Hemisphere, a beautiful spring and summer are predicted for most of South America, and few severe storms are expected to occur. We are expecting no notable deviations from the normal temperatures or precipitation around South America. Hopefully, there will be no serious typhoons in the Pacific nor any strong monsoons in Asia, but at this point, it is impossible to tell. Nothing unusual is foreseen for Australia, New Zealand, or Oceania; each of these places will probably experience their normal weather conditions.

The Almanac will issue one detailed update per week on this website. Click on the links to each area for a more detailed report.

North America   Europe   Asia   Africa   South America   Australia/NZ/Oceania

2 | USING QUANTIFIERS

Read the text of an e-mail from Ricardo to Marco. Complete the e-mail. Circle the correct quantifiers.

Dear Marco,

Well, you certainly seem to be having (a lot of)/ many fun in the United States now. I see that
1.

<u>a few / a little</u> friends in your life makes <u>a number of / a great deal</u> of difference to your state of
2. **3.**

mind. You should send <u>a little / a few</u> news about the lady you wrote about. Is she special, or do
4.

you have <u>many / much</u> girlfriends? You never used to have <u>any / no</u> girlfriends at all, Marco. What
5. **6.**

happened? Did you have <u>a couple of / a bit of</u> luck suddenly? Did you suddenly get handsome? Do
7.

<u>a great deal of / all</u> the girls call you up every day? If you think that I sound jealous, I am.
8.

  <u>A little / A couple of</u> weeks ago you were complaining that <u>either / every</u> person you had met
9. **10.**

was ignoring you; now it seems that you have <u>an amount of / a bunch of</u> friends and that you are
11.

even doing well in <u>a couple of / a bit of</u> your classes. I, on the other hand, may fail
12.

<u>a great deal of / most of</u> my classes. Besides that, I lost <u>a great many / a lot of</u> money last month
13. **14.**

when I invested in a "get-rich-quick" scheme. I borrowed money from everybody, and now I owe

<u>many / a great deal of</u> money to <u>a bit of / a few of</u> our friends.
15. **16.**

  Marco, do you think that you could lend me <u>a little / a few</u> money? I'll pay you back in
17.

<u>a little / a couple of</u> months, I promise.
18.

Your friend,

Ricardo

3 | USING QUANTIFIERS

Aunt Madeline has taken her sister's four children to Big Frank's Franks for a treat. The boys are Adam and Barry, and the girls are Nicole and Zoe. The Xs in the chart below show what each child is having to eat. (XXX = a very large quantity.) Using the information in the chart, complete the sentences below. Use each quantifier in the box only one time.

	ADAM	BARRY	NICOLE	ZOE
hot dog	X X X	X	X	
hamburger				X
fish sandwich				
fries	X	X	X	X
mustard		X	X	X
ketchup	X	X X X		X
salad				X
soda	X, extra large		X, small	
chocolate milkshake		X, medium		X, extra large

a few of	a lot of	all	any	both	~~every~~	many	much	no	one	two

1. _____Every_____ child is having meat for lunch.

2. _____ child is having a fish sandwich.

3. _____ boys are having hot dogs.

4. _____ girl is having a hamburger.

5. _____ the children are having fries.

6. _____ children are having soda.

7. _____ the children are using mustard.

8. Adam is having _____ hot dogs.

9. Nicole isn't drinking _____ soda.

10. Barry is using _____ ketchup on his hot dog.

11. Adam, Barry, and Nicole aren't having _____ salad.

4 | USING QUANTIFIERS

Read this passage from a lecture on the topic of the changing English language. Complete the passage. Circle the correct quantifiers.

Is the English language changing? Yes, and so is (every) / a / one human language.
1.

A few / All / Several language changes, evolves, and adapts to the needs of its users. This is not a
2.

bad thing; in fact, it's a good thing.

For example, in 1950 there were any / no / a little words in English to refer to modems, fax
3.

machines, or cable TV. As long as the needs of language users continue to change, so will the

language. The change is so slow some / each / most year that we hardly notice it. But reading
4.

Shakespeare's writings from the 16th century is very difficult for much / every / most people
5.

today.

Language changes for several / a great deal of / every reasons. First, it changes because the
6.

needs of much / a great many / little speakers change. Each / A couple of / All new product or
7. **8.**

technology or experience requires new words to describe it clearly and efficiently. The fax is an

example. Originally it was called a *facsimile* machine, because it allowed one / both / all person to
9.

send another a facsimile, or copy, of a document. As the machines became more commonplace,

people began using the shorter form *fax* to refer to each / both / a couple of the machine and the
10.

document, as well as to the action of sending a fax.

Another reason for change is that every / some / no two people have had exactly the same
11.

language experience. Every / Some / No person has a slightly different set of words and
12.

constructions, depending on the region he or she comes from; his or her age, work, education level;

etc. We pick up new words and phrases from any of / some / all the different people we talk with.
13.

We get new words from much / a great deal of / many different places. We borrow them from
14.

other languages (*sushi, chutzpah*), we create them by shortening longer words (*gym* from

gymnasium) or by combining words (*brunch* from *breakfast* and *lunch*), and we make them out of

proper names (*Levi's, Fahrenheit*).

What's true of English is true of every / any / all languages: They change. They change less in
15.

a little / a few / every isolated communities, but in most places around the globe, there are
16.

a great deal of / plenty of / any changes going on all the time.
17.

5 | USING QUANTIFIERS

Read this passage about choosing a financial advisor. Complete the passage. Use the words in the box above each section.

Though sometimes it is profitable to manage your own finances, in many cases the advice of an experienced financial planner is in order.

| expertise | ~~financial planner~~ | paycheck | professional advice | time |

Who needs a _____*financial planner*_____ to help plan finances? People whose income
   1.

and assets are more than just a _____ need one. If you don't have any
                                                    2.

_____ because you're too busy, or if, although highly intelligent, you
            3.

have little _____ in the area of money, you may benefit from some
                          4.

_____ .
            5.

| goals | professionals | vacation | year |

Do you want to improve your current financial situation? Do you want to plan for inevitable

future expenses? What about retiring while you're young enough to enjoy it? How about being

able to take a _____ or two every _____? For
                          6.   **7.**

these and many other _____ , you could benefit from the advice of one of
                                      8.

a number of _____ .
                          9.

| experience | interests | money | specialty | stock market | trust | insurance |

What kind of professional? A financial advisor may have one _____ ,
                                                                                          10.

such as _____ . Or he or she may have more _____
                  11.   **12.**

working in the _____ . Whatever the specialty, the advisor must have no
                          13.

financial _____ that conflict with your own. You shouldn't invest too
                    14.

much _____ with the advisor at first. After you feel that the advisor is
                15.

looking out for your financial welfare, you will probably develop a great deal of

_____ in him or her.
            16.

6 | USING QUANTIFIERS

Read this restaurant review. Cross out the phrases that are NOT appropriate for the nouns they modify. Cross out either one or two items in each set of parentheses.

(Many / ~~Much~~ / A lot of) people in our town
1.
have been looking for a good Middle Eastern
restaurant. We have (a few / a little / some)
2.
Italian restaurants in the family style,
(a couple of / a great deal of / every) French
3.
bistros, (several / a few / a little) Asian
4.
restaurants, and (one / some / every) Mexican
5.
restaurant, but we haven't had (no / any / each)
6.
good, authentic Middle Eastern restaurants—
until now.

The new restaurant Sahara has excellent food
and service, along with (some / any / a few)
7.
exotic atmosphere: flowing red curtains,
(plenty of / a great many / a great deal of)
8.
embroidered pillows on the floor, and
(a great deal of / a great many / every) Moroccan
9.
lamps hanging from the ceiling. As soon as we
arrived, we were seated in a roomy booth.
Almost immediately, a waiter brought
(some / a couple of / every) hot pita bread and
10.
(some / one / any) olive oil to dip it in.
11.

To begin, my companion and I chose
(two / one / both) different appetizers: She had
12.
(a little / some / one) stuffed grape leaves, and I
13.
had a plate of creamy hummus and tangy baba
ganoush. (Both / Two / A couple) of them were
14.
delicious. Then, our main courses: the lamb
kabob, which consists of pieces of lamb and
(a few / a little / much) vegetables—onions,
15.
peppers, and mushrooms—which was tender
and tasty, and the chicken, which had been
marinated in a sauce made of (a little / some /
16.
several) mysterious spices, was out of this
world. We both had a side dish consisting of
yogurt with (lots of / several / much) vegetables
17.
cut up in it.

Of course, we wanted dessert, and we chose
the baklava, a flaky pastry filled with
(some / a little / plenty of) pistachio nuts and
18.
covered with (a little / a few / a couple of)
19.
honey.

You'd better get to this restaurant soon. Before
long, when word gets around, there will be a
long wait to get in.

7 | EDITING

A "scam" is a scheme to cheat people. "Spam" is unsolicited e-mail that goes out to large numbers of people. Read the text of an e-mail that is both a scam and spam. There are 14 mistakes in the use of quantifiers. The first mistake is already corrected. Find and correct 13 more. Change only the quantifiers; do not change any other words.

Dear Sir or Madam:

It gives us ~~many~~ *much* pleasure to write this letter to you. Our bank has any information which will benefit you enormously. We are in possession of a great many money in an account with your name on it!!! Yes, this is true. An unnamed person has designated these funds for YOU!

In order to withdraw the money from the bank, we need to request a few information from you:

1. What is your Social Security number? We need this in order to access all account of yours.

2. What is your date of birth and where were you born? We need this information to answer every questions about your identity.

3. Please send the name of your bank and your account number. We need this so we can transfer the money easily without no problems with international banking laws. Please write all number carefully.

4. What is the password for your bank account number? Please double-check this password, and make sure it is up-to-date. A great deal of people have lost out on receiving their money because of incorrectly written passwords.

5. Please take these steps immediately. If the account is not settled by the last day of this month, you will not be able to receive some money.

It has taken a while for us to find you. That's why you must respond quickly in order to meet the deadline for unclaimed funds. Do not take many time to respond or you will lose each of the money in your account!

Also, very important! Please keep this matter confidential. Even if only a little people find out about this, it could make many trouble with the bureaucracy.

Very truly yours,

B.V. Jackson, President

Shady People's Bank, Inc.

8 | PERSONALIZATION

If you won the lottery, what would you do with the money? Write some of your ideas. Use some of the phrases from the box.

> First, I would pay all . . .
>
> I might buy a couple of . . .
>
> Then I would put a little . . .
>
> I would contribute to certain . . .
>
> I would invest in some . . .
>
> I would finally have enough . . .
>
> I would take a few . . .
>
> I would give some . . .
>
> I would buy many . . .
>
> I would relax and have a lot of . . .

Modification of Nouns

1 | ORDERING MODIFIERS

Read this review of a fashion show. Complete the review by putting the modifiers in parentheses in the correct order. Place commas where they are needed.

Last week at the _____*annual fashion*_____ show in Paris, some _____
          1. (fashion / annual)   **2. (young / bright)**

designers displayed their latest creations. Everybody had expected these _____
                                                  3. (spring / new)

fashions to be similar to last year's rather ordinary and boring clothes; instead, the designers delighted

the audience with a brilliant presentation. Drawing on _____ inspirations,
                                         4. (various / international)

they showed the first _____ collection in a decade.
                      5. (big / exciting)

Maurice Isak's inspiration came from the Orient; his _____ lines with
                                        6. (straight / long)

only the _____ ornamentation, done in _____
           7. (added / smallest)   **8. (expensive / silk)**

fabrics, obviously recalled some _____ paintings. He translated these
                              9. (Japanese / old)

_____ images into _____ suits and gave them
     10. (classic / beautiful)   **11. (elegant / business)**

a _____ touch. Another designer, Louis Darrieux, had apparently visited
  12. (fabulous / modern)

Tahiti, as evidenced by his _____ outfits, which bring to mind images of
                            13. (brightly colored / wild)

_____ islands and which are perfect in _____
   14. (tropical / South Sea)   **15. (summer / casual)**

clothes. But inspiration for the _____ clothes came from sunny Spain, in
                           16. (liveliest / new)

Guillermo Pérez's collection. Those _____ hues combined with several
                            17. (pink / hot)

_____ colors woven together with turquoise and orange in
    18. (purple / brilliant)

_____ skirts were the sensation of the show.
    19. (cotton / long)

It has been a long time since we have seen such beautiful styles from any

_____ designer; we are pleased as punch to have these
20. (well-known / contemporary)

_____ artists among us.
    21. (new / fabulous)

2 | USING NOUN MODIFIERS

Read this passage from a memoir. Turn the phrases in the box into noun modifier constructions. Then complete the passage by writing the modifiers in the appropriate blanks.

a house for dogs	a night in the summer
a pie made of peaches	a sister who is a baby
a table in the kitchen	cats that live in the house
dogs that belong to a family	dreams from childhood
gardens where flowers grow	gardens where vegetables grow
horses displayed in shows	horses used for work
jam made of strawberries	memories of childhood
tea made of blackberries	~~trees that grow apples~~

My happiest memories are of visiting my grandparents' farm every summer when I was a

child. There they had many _____ apple trees _____ that I used to climb to pick the apples.
                                         1.

They had both _____, where roses and violets grew, and
                        2.

_____, from which we gathered the carrots and beans that we ate at
          3.

dinner.

There were some horses—_____—which helped my grandfather and
                                    4.

the men in the fields, and even a few _____, which won prizes in the state
                                              5.

fairs. There were a lot of cats, but they weren't _____; they roamed
                                                        6.

outside, particularly in the barn area, hunting the mice. There were always the beloved

_____, too, that patrolled the fields and protected us from intruders.
          7.

Usually they slept outside in the special _____ that Grandfather had
                                                  8.

made, but Pluto, my favorite, was allowed to sleep on my bed.

My grandmother used to make her own jellies and jams; I loved to pick the strawberries in the

fields to make my contribution to her special _____. She also made a
                                                      9.

delicious tea from the wild blackberries growing nearby. I would have that wonderful

_____ at night, along with a piece of _____ that
          10.   **11.**

she made from her own home-grown peaches. We would sit at the _____
                                                                          12.

after clearing off the dinner dishes and talk about life, about her _____ of

13.

so many years earlier and about my _____ for the future. Then she would

14.

gently lead me to the small, cozy bedroom that I shared with my _____,

15.

who was too young then to appreciate the beautiful times with my grandmother. I slept soundly

and peacefully every _____ that I spent at my grandparents' house, and I

16.

dreamed almost every night in the intervening winters that I was basking in the warmth of her love.

3 | FORMING COMPOUND MODIFIERS

Read this list of items recently purchased at Joseph and Lillian's Antique Shop. Rewrite the
items as nouns with modifiers. Each item will include a compound modifier.

Joseph and Lillian's Antique Shop

1. 2 silver candlesticks   95 years old

   2 ninety-five-year-old silver candlesticks _____

2. 1 dining room table   200 years old

_____

3. 8 dining room chairs   covered in velvet

_____

4. 2 Tiffany lamps   century old

_____

5. 1 samovar   plated in silver

_____

(continued)

6. 2 rocking chairs   150 years old

_____

_____

7. 1 Persian carpet   woven by hand

_____

_____

8. 1 manuscript   written by hand

_____

_____

9. 3 coffee tables   inlaid with ivory

_____

_____

10. 4 serving dishes   painted by hand

_____

_____

11. 2 mahogany beds   carved by hand

_____

_____

12. 2 vases   130 years old / inlaid with gold

_____

_____

4 | USING NOUN MODIFIERS

Read this excerpt from a graduate school application. Turn the phrases in the box into noun modifier constructions. Then complete the excerpt by writing the modifiers in the appropriate blanks.

activities for students who are international	award from five states for volunteerism
award given for four years of service	~~camp where boys go in the summer~~
council for ethics of students	disorder that is a deficit in paying attention
houses that are old and dilapidated	local shop for coffee

I hope to enrich my life by attending the John K. Smith School of Business. There, I will grow and refine my abilities by enhancing the knowledge I already have about business. I am bringing a lot of leadership experience to the school, and sincere eagerness to learn. During the past five years, I have been active in community and university activities, and I have won several awards. I have been:

1. a tennis coach at a _____*boys'*_____ / _____*summer*_____ / _____*camp*_____.

2. the weekend manager at a _____ / _____ / _____.

3. the president of the _____ / _____ / _____ for ethical behavior at my university.

4. the coordinator of the _____ / _____ / _____ for foreign students at my university.

5. a volunteer who fixes up _____ / _____ / _____ for the Better Community Housing Commission.

6. a volunteer who works in the public school system with children who have _____ / _____ / _____.

7. the recipient of the _____ - _____ / _____ / _____, in appreciation for service during four years of undergraduate school.

8. the recipient of the _____ - _____ / _____ / _____, for the most valuable contributions to volunteerism in five states.

I hope I can further broaden my career and my life by attending your school. If I am fortunate enough to do so, I expect to make the John K. Smith School of Business proud of me as a graduate.

I am looking forward to hearing from you soon.

Very truly yours,

Edward J. Larson

Edward T. Larson

5 | EDITING

Read this passage about a writer's first days in New York. There are 18 mistakes in the use of noun modifiers. The first mistake is already corrected. Find and correct 17 more.

Moving from the ~~country fresh~~ *fresh country* air to the head-clogging, polluted stuff that city dwellers breathe presents a shock to the body. Ten years ago, I had miraculously obtained a well-paying job in the publishing glamorous world, and I moved with my wife and two daughters from southwest beautiful Montana with its blue clear skies to New York, where there appeared to us to be no skies at all, only gray dirty smog.

Within a week, my wife and children and I all came down with a respiratory mysterious ailment. Coughing and sneezing, with eyes and noses dripping, we suffered for 10 days. A 10-days siege in a small four-room apartment felt like being imprisoned in a cement, cold jail cell. We were accustomed to being outdoors, in the open Montana air. After only two weeks at my new prized job, I had to call in sick. And was I sick! My 42-years-old, feverish body ached as it never had ached before. Iron gigantic hammers pounded in my head. My lungs felt like lead huge weights. I coughed constantly, so that I never had more than a two-hours rest, even though I took double the recommended dose of the cough over-the-counter medicine we had bought at the drug corner store. Finally, after 10 days, we recovered physically, although not psychologically, from our New York rude reception. My first three weeks in the Big Apple gave me the feeling that I lived in a foreign and hostile country—and it took many months until I felt differently. Now I love New York. I love to breathe the New York wonderful air, and you couldn't get me to live any place else.

6 | PERSONALIZATION

What do you expect or hope that you, your family, and your friends will be doing in five years? In 10 years? When you or they are 65 years old? Select one or more people from each group (1–3) below and write a few sentences about each person. Use as many of the types of modifiers from the box as you can.

1. myself / my mother / my sister / my wife / my daughter / my best female friend

2. myself / my father / my brother / my husband / my son / my best male friend

3. my parents / my brothers and sisters / my children / my best friends

TYPES OF MODIFIERS	
Determiners	a, an, the, this, those, his, her, their
Quantifiers	one, two, few, little, many, some
Adjectives	of opinion (nice); size (big); age (old); etc.
Nouns	apple tree, shoe store, six-lane highway

Example

In five years, I expect that I will be living with my wife in an upscale two-bedroom apartment in this town. We may have one baby by that time, and we'll be planning to move into a larger place—maybe an old country house. In about 10 years, we'll be at the peak of our careers and will probably have two healthy, beautiful children. Since we expect to make a lot of money, we'll be able to retire long before age 65, and we'll be experienced world travelers.

1. _____

_____

_____

_____

2. _____

_____

_____

_____

3. _____

_____

_____

_____

UNIT

11 Adjective Clauses: Review and Expansion

1 | RECOGNIZING ADJECTIVE CLAUSES

Read this article about an invention and its inventor. There are 23 adjective clauses. The first one is already underlined. Find and underline 22 more. (Remember that some adjective clauses do not have a relative pronoun.)

◼ LIQUID PAPER ◼

This is the story of a very simple invention <u>that you can find in almost every office in the whole world today</u>. It is also the story of an inventor whose creativity and persistence resulted in a very useful product. What is the famous invention? It is Liquid Paper, the white liquid that covers up the mistakes you make when writing or typing. It was invented in the early 1950s by Bette Nesmith Graham, a secretary in Dallas, Texas, who began using tempera paint to cover up the typing errors in her work.

At the time, Ms. Nesmith was a 27-year-old single mother of one son, struggling to make ends meet and working as a secretary to the chairman of a big Dallas bank. When she began to work with her first electric typewriter, she found that the type marks she typed onto the paper didn't erase as cleanly as those from manual typewriters. So Ms. Nesmith, who was also an artist, quietly began painting out her mistakes. Soon she was supplying bottles of her homemade preparation, which she called Mistake Out, to other secretaries in the building.

When she lost her job with the company, Ms. Nesmith turned to working full time to develop the Mistake Out as a business, expanding from her house into a small trailer she had bought for the backyard. In hopes of marketing her product, she approached IBM, which turned her down. She stepped up her own marketing and within a decade was a financial success. The product, which came to be called Liquid Paper, was manufactured in four countries and sold in nearly three dozen. In fiscal 1979, which ended about six months before she sold the company, it had sales of $38 million, of which $3.5 million was net income. By the time Ms. Nesmith finally sold her business to Gillette in 1979, she had built her simple, practical idea into a $47.5 million business.

It is heartwarming that the story has a happy ending in more ways than one. Ms. Nesmith remarried and became Mrs. Graham. Her son, Michael, a musician of whom she was understandably proud, became very successful as one of the members of a music group called the Monkees, which appeared on an NBC television show for several years in the mid-1960s. Subsequently a country-rock musician, a songwriter, and a video producer, he now heads a production company in California, where he also directs some charities.

With some of her profits, Mrs. Graham established a foundation whose purpose is to provide leading intellectuals with the time, space, and compatible colleagues that they need to ponder and articulate the most important social problems of our era. Bette Nesmith Graham first developed a product that there was clearly a need for; then she used the substantial profits for charitable purposes, which is a fine thing to do.

The story of Liquid Paper and Bette Nesmith Graham is a story everyone can appreciate. It shows how a wonderful product came to market because of the cleverness and perseverance of its inventor. Perhaps you, too, have a clever idea that will spread like wildfire if only you can give it the kind of spark that Mrs. Graham gave to her product.

2 | USING RELATIVE PRONOUNS

Read this essay from a university composition class. Complete the essay. Circle the correct relative pronouns, or — if no relative pronoun is needed.

THE TEACHER WHO INFLUENCED MY LIFE THE MOST

School was always very important to me. Therefore, it is not surprising that the person which / (who) influenced my life the most was a teacher. In my 12 years of school, I have had many
1.
teachers (whom) / which I have admired greatly, but Mrs. Thompson, that / who was my French
2. **3.**
teacher in the 10th grade, is the teacher to whom / that I owe the most.
4.

(continued)

Mrs. Thompson was an excellent teacher, and I really liked the way she taught the class. It was a class where / which I felt important. In this class, I was able to excel, that / which helped
5. **6.**
me feel better about myself. Before I took this class, I was not the kind of person whom / who
7.
spoke up in groups. In fact, I was very quiet and did not socialize much. Because of the success whose / — I had in this class, though, I became more confident and at ease, something
8.
when / which also helped me to do better in my other classes. I became a better student and a
9.
better person.

My family did not have a lot of money, and it looked like I wasn't going to be able to attend the university. However, Mrs. Thompson wrote strong letters recommending me for scholarships, whom / which I submitted along with the applications. In the end, I was able to get a scholarship
10.
to attend the university. After my acceptance arrived, Mrs. Thompson gave me advice regarding the classes I would take, as well as other academic matters. Those days at the beginning of my college career were difficult for me. They were days when / which I really needed someone's advice,
11.
and Mrs. Thompson came through for me.

My final reason for choosing Mrs. Thompson is the subject to that / which she introduced me.
12.
This was my first class in French, a language that / whose I really liked to study. I enjoyed French
13.
so much that I then took another language—Spanish—the next year. I enjoyed studying both languages and had excellent grades in all my language classes, an accomplishment — / that has
14.
given me the idea of becoming a language teacher myself. I can only hope that I will one day be able to teach as well as Mrs. Thompson, whom / whose class had such a positive impact on my
15.
life.

3 | USING RELATIVE PRONOUNS

Read these job advertisements from the classified section of a newspaper. Complete the ads. Circle the correct relative pronouns.

——————————————— **SECRETARY** ———————————————

Computer Future is looking for a person that / which / whom has the right skills for a fast-paced,
1.
growing office. The current position, that / which / whose is being announced here for the first time,
2.
is for a front-office secretary. Thus, we are looking for a person who can perform secretarial duties

and work with the public. The ideal candidate for this position is someone which / **who** / whom can
3.

type at least 80 wpm and is comfortable with basic and advanced word processing programs. Our

company stresses excellent customer relations, so only those applicants that / who / **whose**
4.

people skills are truly outstanding should apply; an outgoing personality is a requirement. We offer

a very competitive salary, full health insurance, a generous retirement plan, and opportunities for

professional growth, a package of that / **which** / whom other companies can only be envious. If you
5.

think you are the right person for this job, we urge you to apply today.

——————————— **BILINGUAL TELEPHONE OPERATOR** ———————————

A large multinational company seeks an energetic individual which / who / whom has a good
6.

telephone voice. Applicants that / which / whose English and Spanish skills are impeccable should
7.

call Mr. Wilford at 555-1417 to set up an appointment. In addition, we seek someone

when / which / who is familiar with a traditional switchboard but where / which / who also knows
8.   **9.**

how to operate a computer-driven switchboard. In particular, applicants who / whom / whose are
10.

good with details are encouraged to apply. The next two years will be a time when / which / who
11.

our company is expanding rapidly, and similar jobs may be opening up in the very near future;

interested persons should call for a job interview ASAP.

——————————————— **WEB PAGE DESIGNER** ———————————————

Our downtown office is looking for a creative person where / who / whom can meet work
12.

deadlines. The ideal person for this job is someone when / which / who can translate a client's
13.

ideas and needs into a dynamic Web page. We need a designer that / which / whose imagination
14.

can help turn mundane Web pages into innovative sites. In addition, we are looking for a person

who / whom / whose knows HTML and JAVA, programming languages that / where / whose our
15.   **16.**

company uses extensively. If interested, you should submit a detailed résumé, a small portfolio of

previous Web creations, and three letters of reference from clients for which / who / whom you
17.

have worked within the last five years.

4 | USING RELATIVE PRONOUNS

Read this article from a newsletter. Complete the article, using the relative pronouns in the box. Write — if no relative pronoun is needed. Where more than one selection is possible, write all the possibilities.

| that | when | where | which | who | whom | whose | — |

HEALTHY LIFESTYLES BULLETIN

It's Cold Season Again!

Dr. Jennifer Wise has obtained a grant of $17 million for her research on the factors affecting the natural resistance ___*that / which / —*___
1.
the human body has to cold viruses. Dr. Wise has investigated the common beliefs to ___*which*___ people have
2.
long subscribed—for example, the beliefs that colds come from sitting in places

_____ there is a draft,
3.
not wearing warm enough clothing, and sitting

near a person _____
4.
is coughing and sneezing.

She finds no evidence that these factors have much merit, but says that there are other factors

_____ actually
5.
contribute to catching a cold. For example, you can catch a cold from a person

_____ you have been
6.
near just from touching him or her or something

_____ he or she has
7.
touched, so it is very important and effective to wash you hands frequently and well. This is the

most important thing _____
8.
you can do to avoid catching cold.

Additionally, not getting the rest

_____ your body
9.
needs lowers resistance. People

_____ sleep patterns
10.
don't provide them with enough deep sleep will more easily catch a cold than will people

_____ get enough
11.
rest. Deep sleep is especially important at times

_____ people are
12.
under more stress than usual.

As for treating the common cold: Nothing will cure it, but there are some steps

_____ may be taken
13.
to lessen the symptoms. You may take aspirin and other medications

_____ act to relieve
14.
your discomfort, stay in bed if you can, drink plenty of liquids, and partake of the home

remedy _____ has
15.
been around for centuries: the chicken soup

_____ your mother makes.
16.

5 | FORMING ADJECTIVE CLAUSES

Read this passage about the Meyers-Briggs Personality Inventory. Complete the passage by writing adjective clauses based on the sentences in parentheses. Sometimes more than one relative pronoun is correct, and sometimes a relative pronoun may be omitted.

Of all the personality measurement instruments that exist today, perhaps the Meyers-Briggs Personality Inventory is the most well known. It is used extensively by human resources departments in an effort to help them understand the people who work in their company.

What is the Meyers-Briggs Personality Inventory? Simply put, the Meyers-Briggs is a test

which/that indicates an individual's personality type . According to this test, there are four main
    1. (The test indicates an individual's personality type.)

dimensions, or types, of personality. For each dimension, there are two categories.

The first dimension is a basic one: extrovert or introvert. An extrovert is a person

_____. An extrovert is not very
    2. (This person feels energized around others.)

comfortable or productive being alone. In contrast, an introvert is a person

_____. An introvert feels
    3. (This person's energies are activated by being alone.)

most comfortable when he or she is alone.

The second dimension is connected to how a person notices and remembers

information. Some people in this category are referred to as sensors: those

_____. They rely on their past
    4. (These people pay attention to details in the world.)

experiences and knowledge of how science works to make objective determinations.

Sensors are very practical people. In contrast, an intuitive is an individual

_____. Intuitives usually focus on what will
    5. (The individual is more interested in relationships between people and things.)

probably be a successful move, mostly because they sense it is what people want. They are

sensitive to other people's feelings and act accordingly.

The third personality dimension _____ is that of
    6. (This test measures this dimension.)

thinker or feeler. Have you ever had a boss _____?
    7. (Your boss made decisions objectively.)

Maybe you thought some of his or her decisions were cold or impersonal. Perhaps they were.

Perhaps your boss was a person _____
    8. (The person's primary way to reach a conclusion was this:)

to determine what makes sense and what is logical. That boss was not a person

_____. Your boss was a thinker, not a feeler.
    9. (The person took other people's feelings into consideration.)

(continued)

A feeler, unlike that boss, makes decisions based on his or her own personal values and the

feelings _____ about the anticipated results of
10. (He or she has feelings.)

those decisions.

The final dimension deals with the type of environment in

_____: planned or unplanned. Judgers are
11. (We prefer to live or work in this type of environment.)

people _____; they judge, or anticipate,
12. (People prefer a planned and predictable environment.)

what is going to happen and try to live their lives in accordance with these plans.

In contrast, perceivers are more interested in keeping their options open. They want to be able

to respond to the needs of the situation and the moment

_____. Are you the kind of person
13. (They find themselves in the situation and the moment.)

_____, or do you prefer to take life one day
14. (The person's life must be planned in advance.)

at a time and have some room for spontaneity?

A test such as the Meyers-Briggs may help determine what type of personality an employee

has and the spot _____. At the same time,
15. (He should be placed here to most enhance the company.)

you as an employee might benefit from a test like this because you might find the place in

_____.
16. (You would be the happiest and most productive here.)

6 | DISTINGUISHING BETWEEN IDENTIFYING AND NON-IDENTIFYING CLAUSES

*Read this information about the Moonrise Film Festival. Each numbered sentence contains
an identifying or non-identifying adjective clause. For each sentence, circle the letter of the
correct statement about the modified noun. Pay special attention to punctuation.*

1. Moviegoers, who appreciate fine films, were very satisfied with the Moonrise Film Festival
   this year.

   a. Moviegoers in general appreciate fine films.

   b. Only some moviegoers appreciate fine films.

2. Moviegoers who appreciate fine films were very satisfied with the Moonrise Film Festival
   this year.

   a. Only some moviegoers appreciate fine films.

   b. Moviegoers in general appreciate fine films.

3. The films, which were chosen for their artistry in cinematography, left vivid and lasting impressions.

   a. The films in general left vivid and lasting impressions.

   b. Only some films left vivid and lasting impressions.

4. The films that were chosen for their artistry in cinematography left vivid and lasting impressions.

   a. Only some films left vivid and lasting impressions.

   b. The films in general left vivid and lasting impressions.

5. Offbeat films brought critical acclaim to directors who are normally very profit oriented.

   a. Directors in general are normally very profit oriented.

   b. Only some directors are normally very profit oriented.

6. In the animation category, the audience was surprised and satisfied by Hollywood's new-style cartoons, which address serious social concerns.

   a. Only some of Hollywood's new-style cartoons address social concerns.

   b. Hollywood's new-style cartoons in general address social concerns.

7. The foreign entries, which were brilliantly directed, unfortunately may not succeed at the box office here.

   a. The foreign entries in general were brilliantly directed.

   b. Only some of the foreign entries were brilliantly directed.

8. Only the documentaries, which proved to be disappointing this year, represented a poor selection.

   a. The documentaries in general were a poor selection.

   b. Only some of the documentaries were a poor selection.

9. We hope to see further entries from the African countries whose film industries are just emerging.

   a. The film industries in African countries in general are just emerging.

   b. The film industries in some African countries are just emerging.

10. If such excellence in selection and presentation continues, the Moonrise Film Festival will soon take its place among the film festivals of the world that rival Cannes.

    a. Film festivals in general rival Cannes.

    b. Only some film festivals rival Cannes.

7 | EDITING

Read this passage about ways to categorize people. There are 17 mistakes in the use of adjective clauses. The first mistake is already corrected. Find and correct 16 more.

               which

One of the ways in ~~whom~~ people can be classified is by labeling them *extroverts* or *introverts*. However, there are other methods, some of them are now considered to have little scientific value, that people use to conveniently categorize members of the human race.

For example, there is the division into mesomorphs, who are muscular; endomorphs, who tend to be fat; and ectomorphs, who are thin. The endomorph is stereotyped as a relaxed person without obsessions, whereas the ectomorph is stereotyped as a person whom is nervous and serious and who rarely smiles.

Another easily made division defines people as Type A and Type B. Type A is the category to whom people belong if they are very serious, ambitious, and driven. Type A originally described people, usually middle-aged males, whom suffered a lot of heart attacks. Type B, on the other hand, labels a rather passive, ambitionless person of that others frequently take advantage, and which is probably not a candidate for a heart attack.

Some people categorize human beings by the astrological sign that they were born under it. For example, a person who born between April 22 and May 21 is called a Taurus and is supposed to possess certain characteristics, such as congeniality and tact. A person that born between June 22 and July 21 is a Cancer and is reputed to be stubborn but effective. There are 12 such categories, which encompass all the months of the year. Many people base their lives and relationships on the predictions what are made by astrologers.

One recent theory to categorize people is the theory of left-brained and right-brained people. According to this theory, right-brained people, that are intuitive and romantic, are the artists and creative people of the world. Left-brained people, who they are logical in their thinking, turn out to be mathematicians and scientists. According to this theory, people whose their abilities are not developed enough in certain areas can develop the side of the brain they want to improve it in order to better balance their personality.

All of these theories, which in themselves are too simplistic, are indeed unscientific. However, they have provided attractive and sometimes amusing solutions for people are looking for easy ways to understand the human race. Different theories of categorizing people, which it is always a difficult thing to do, will continue to come and go.

8 | PERSONALIZATION

What is your concept of the ideal teacher and the ideal student? In one paragraph, write a description of the kind of teacher you like best. In a second paragraph, imagine that you are a teacher. What kind of student would you prefer to have? Use some of the phrases from the boxes, appropriately finished with adjective clauses.

> **The Ideal Teacher**
>
> I like a teacher who . . .
>
> I would rather have a teacher to whom . . .
>
> It's important to be taught by someone whose . . .
>
> The teacher would use instructional materials that . . .
>
> There will be times when . . .

> **The Ideal Student**
>
> The ideal student is a person . . .
>
> The ideal student is someone whose . . .
>
> This is a person for whom . . .
>
> The student will have free time that he or she . . .
>
> As a teacher, I would prefer to have students I . . .

_____

_____

_____

_____

_____

_____

_____

_____

12 Adjective Clauses with Prepositions; Adjective Phrases

1 | IDENTIFYING ADJECTIVE CLAUSES AND ADJECTIVE PHRASES

Read this wedding announcement from The Sunday Times. *There are 11 adjective clauses and 6 adjective phrases. The first of each is already marked. Find and underline 10 more adjective clauses. Find and circle 5 more adjective phrases.*

The Sunday Times

Wedding Announcements

Carolina Manning, a daughter of Dr. and Mrs. John Manning of Boston, was married on Sunday to Matthias Wolfe, the son of Dr. Maria and Mr. Douglas Wolfe of New York. Reverend Harry Carter performed the ceremony at the All-Faiths Religious Center in Boston.

Ms. Manning will continue to use her name professionally. She is well-known as the originator of the children's television show *Hot Ice Cream*, of which she is both the writer and producer. She has a degree in film studies from the University of Southern California and she also received a master's degree in cinematography from New York University. Her father, whose text on Shakespeare is required reading in many colleges, is a professor of English at Boston University, at which he holds the John B. Baker Chair of English Literature. Her mother taught in the public school system for 30 years, the last 20 of which were at Grisham High School, where she was principal. She retired last June.

Mr. Wolfe is a law clerk in the office of Superior Court Judge Ruth Heller, for whom he had worked during the two previous summers. He has a degree in Public Administration from Syracuse University, from which he graduated magna cum laude, and a law degree from Boston University. His father is an editor at Koala Publications, a children's book publisher. His mother, Dr. Maria Lopez Wolfe, is a pediatrician currently serving as Chief of Pediatrics at Children's Hospital.

The bride and bridegroom met at the Woodland Fire Department last November, while waiting in a long line to vote. They soon discovered that they had common values, many of which are political. Ms. Manning is active in the Southside Independent Voters Caucus, dedicated to informing citizens about current issues. Mr. Wolfe occasionally publishes his letters of opinion, some of which have drawn national attention, in the Beacon Globe.

Ms. Manning will be known socially as Mrs. Wolfe. The couple, several of whose friends and colleagues live in the same wooded complex, will reside in Contemplation Woods, near the fire department at which they first met.

2 | FORMING ADJECTIVE CLAUSES WITH QUANTIFIERS

Read the boldfaced statements and guess whether they are **True** *or* **False**. *Circle your answers. Then read the explanations that follow. Complete the explanations by writing adjective clauses using the words in parentheses plus a preposition and a relative pronoun.*

1. **The flu vaccine can give you the flu.**   TRUE / (FALSE)

   The flu vaccine is made from killed viruses that are not infectious. However, there could

   be side effects, _____*some of which are*_____ fever, aches and soreness, and
                      (some / are)

   swelling or redness at the site of the injection. These symptoms should only last for about

   a day.

2. **Arthritis is affected by changes in the weather.**   TRUE / FALSE

   This has only recently been backed up by science. There have been several studies on this

   subject, _____ by Tufts University. The researchers found
             (one / was done recently)

   the nearest weather station for each participant in the study and monitored different weather

   conditions. They discovered that cooler temperatures and changes in barometric pressure

   affected the participants, _____ increased arthritis pain
               (almost all / suffered)

   with stormy and cooler weather.

3. **You should leave a cut or wound uncovered. It will heal faster that way.**   TRUE / FALSE

   Many people think that you should let a wound get air for it to heal faster. But in fact the

   best way to aid healing is to keep antibacterial ointments on the cut, which will speed up

   healing and reduce scarring. These ointments, _____
                              (most / are available)

   over-the-counter in pharmacies, should be applied after the wound is cleaned and the skin

   has dried.

   (continued)

4. **Exercising at night will disrupt your sleep.**   TRUE / FALSE

Many people think that working out before bed will make it difficult to fall asleep.

However, recent studies show that participants, _____,

(the majority / were physically fit)

found that night-time workouts did not harm, and even may have improved, their quality

of sleep.

5. **Women who lift weights will get bulky muscles.**   TRUE / FALSE

According to some experts, women, _____ the

(most / do not have)

necessary amount of testosterone for extreme muscle-building, will not develop large, bulky

muscles from weight-lifting. Strength training alone will not cause women to build these

muscles, although the use of steroids might.

6. **Vitamins from supplements are absorbed as well as vitamins from foods.**   TRUE / FALSE

Vitamins, _____ quite well from vitamin pills, are

(all / are absorbed)

helpful to maintain optimum nutrition. In some cases, supplements are absorbed at even

higher rates than vitamins occurring naturally in foods. For example, folic acid supplements

are absorbed more efficiently than folic acid from foods. This is important for women,

_____ high needs for this vitamin.

(many / have)

7. **Low-fat or nonfat means no calories.**   TRUE / FALSE

Everyone knows that fruits and vegetables, _____

(most / are)

naturally low in fat and calories, are healthful. However, foods whose labels claim that they

are low-fat or nonfat may still have a lot of calories because manufacturers often add sugar,

flour, or starch to make them taste better. These additives still have calories and cause the

products, _____ "low-fat" or "nonfat," to have about the

(all / are labeled)

same or more calories than a product not making this claim.

8. **The older you get, the fewer hours of sleep you need.**   TRUE / FALSE

Sleep experts recommend a range of seven to nine hours of sleep for the average adult.

While sleep patterns change as people age, the need for a good night's sleep,

_____, is important for good health at any age.

(the amount / doesn't change)

3 | REDUCING ADJECTIVE CLAUSES TO ADJECTIVE PHRASES

Read these movie descriptions from a TV program guide. Complete the sentences by writing adjective phrases or the beginnings of adjective phrases based on the adjective clauses in parentheses.

1. **Planet of the Apes.** This remake of the 1960s classic is spectacular. After flying through a "worm hole" in space, an astronaut (Mark Wahlberg) crashes on a planet where apes rule over humans. He is aided by a sympathetic chimpanzee,

    played by Helena Bonham Carter , as he leads a small band
    (who is played by Helena Bonham Carter)
    of rebels against their captors.

2. **Finding Nemo.** Don't miss the adventures of Marlin, an overprotective clown fish

    _____. When he hooks up with a
    (who is looking for his missing son)
    funny tang fish in the search, the laughs don't stop. Brilliant animation with the voices

    of Albert Brooks and Ellen DeGeneres.

3. **Beauty and the Beast.** Disney's dazzling musical tells of the romance between a beautiful

    young woman and a prince _____.
    (who has been transformed by a magic spell)

4. **The Last Samurai.** With gorgeous visuals of Japan in the 1870s, this is the story of Capt.

    Nathan Algren, an American military officer hired by the Emperor of Japan. Algren,

    _____, undergoes a spiritual
    (who is brilliantly portrayed by Tom Cruise)
    rebirth during his encounters with the Samurai.

5. **The X-Files.** FBI agents Mulder and Scully seek the truth about conspiracies,

    extraterrestrials, and mysterious black oozing liquid in this thriller mystery,

    _____.
    (which was adapted from the TV series)

6. **Deliverance.** Four men on a canoe trip struggle for survival. In a thrilling adventure

    _____, each of the men
    (which has turned into a nightmare)
    undergoes a change of character. Burt Reynolds stars.

(continued)

7. Diamonds are Forever. This is Sean Connery's sixth appearance as James Bond in a thriller

_____ on the trail of stolen gems.
     (that zips him from Amsterdam to Las Vegas)

8. Titanic. The Oscar-winning blockbuster, _____

     (which stars Leonardo DiCaprio and Kate Winslet)

as star-crossed lovers aboard the doomed ship, provides a moving story and

amazing visual effects.

9. Star Wars Episode II: Attack of the Clones. The saga about a faraway galaxy continues.

Anakin Skywalker (Hayden Christensen) makes progress in his Jedi training, falls in love

with the beautiful Queen Amidala (Natalie Portman), and grows into a young man

_____ .

     (who is capable of a power that may destroy him)

10. The Godfather, _____ of a story

     (which is Francis Ford Coppola's Oscar-winning version)

about a power struggle among organized-crime factions in the 1940s, stars Marlon

Brando, Al Pacino, and James Caan.

4 | FORMING SENTENCES WITH ADJECTIVE CLAUSES AND ADJECTIVE PHRASES

Combine these pairs of sentences to make single sentences. Use adjective phrases,
adjective clauses, or adjective clauses with quantifiers.

Cinema Pubs: A New Experience in Moviegoing

1. Cinema pubs are small. Being small gives you a more intimate relationship to the film.

   Cinema pubs are small, giving you a more intimate relationship to the film.

2. Cinema pubs contain independent sections of tables and comfortable swivel chairs. This
   allows you to feel like you are in your own living room.

   _____

   _____

3. Servers come to each table before the movie begins and take orders for food and beverages.
   Most of the servers are local college students.

   _____

   _____

4. The ambience in the theater is similar to that in a cabaret. In a cabaret, there is an intimate feeling.

_____

_____

5. In accordance with the cozy atmosphere, the cinema pubs show small films. Many of the small films are from other countries.

_____

_____

6. Although you have come to the theater to see a movie, you will also find that the cinema pub is a gathering place. People like to socialize here.

_____

_____

7. The idea of the cinema pub is beginning to catch on in the United States. The idea of a cinema pub is already popular in the United Kingdom.

_____

_____

8. Cinema pubs show recent films in a relaxed atmosphere. This makes them a welcome alternative to huge and impersonal movie multiplexes.

_____

_____

9. For a change of pace, see your next film at a cinema pub. See the film at the cinema pub that is nearest to you.

_____

_____

5 | EDITING

Read this passage about filmmaking. There are 15 mistakes in the use of adjective clauses and phrases. The first mistake is already corrected. Find and correct 14 more. Delete, fix, or replace words, but do not change punctuation or add words.

After World War II, Europe was the center of important developments in filmmaking, which

~~they~~ strongly influenced motion pictures worldwide. In Italy, well-known movies, some of them

were Rossellini's *Open City*, making in 1945, and De Sica's *Shoeshine* (1946) and *The Bicycle*

(continued)

Thief (1948), established a trend toward realism in film. These directors weren't concerned with contrived plots or stories that produced for entertainment value alone; they took their cameras into the streets to make films showed the harshness of life in the years after the war.

In the next decades, Federico Fellini—was an outstanding director—combined realistic plots with poetic imagery, symbolism, and philosophical ideas in now-classic films, the most famous of them is *La Strada*, which a movie ostensibly about circus people in the streets but really about the meaning of life.

In France, a group of young filmmakers, calling the "New Wave," appeared during the 1950s. This group developed a new kind of focus, which stressed characterization rather than plot and featured new camera and acting techniques, seeing in movies such as Truffaut's *400 Blows*.

In England, another group of filmmakers, was known as the "Angry Young Man" movement, developed a new realism. In Sweden, Ingmar Bergman used simple stories and allegories to look at complex philosophical and social issues, some of them are masterfully explored in *The Seventh Seal*. The Spaniard Luis Buñuel depicted social injustices and used surrealistic techniques, creating films like *Viridiana*.

Postwar developments in filmmaking were not limited to Western Europe. The Japanese director Akira Kurosawa, was the first Asian filmmaker to have a significant influence in Europe, made *Rashomon* in 1950. Movies from India, like Satyajit Ray's *Pather Panchali*, showed us life on the subcontinent. Even in Russia, where filmmaking was under state control, it was possible to make movies like *The Cranes Are Flying*, portray the problems of the individual. Russian directors also made films based on literary classics, included Shakespeare's plays and Tolstoy's monumental historical novel, *War and Peace*.

In summary, in the decades after World War II, filmmaking turned in new directions, as shown by a wide range of movies from around the world, many of them focused on the meaning of life and how to interpret it.

6 | PERSONALIZATION

What was the best movie that you have ever seen? What can you remember about it?
Write two or three paragraphs about the movie. Begin with the sentence, "One of my
favorite movies is . . . ." Use some of the phrases in the box.

> I liked the movie for a number of reasons, some of which are . . .
>
> The movie had some good actors, including . . .
>
> The movie had some really exciting (funny) scenes, examples of which are . . .
>
> I remember the scene taking place . . .
>
> There was an exciting (funny / romantic) plot involving . . .
>
> The movie had an interesting ending, resulting in . . .
>
> The director was _____, also known for directing . . .
>
> I like his (her) movies, all of which . . .
>
> The movie won some awards, including . . .
>
> I would have no trouble recommending this movie, one of the . . .
>
> Perhaps this movie will be shown again soon, in which case . . .

_____

_____

_____

_____

_____

_____

_____

_____

_____

_____

_____

_____

_____

_____

Workbook Answer Key

In this answer key, where the contracted form is given, the full form is often also correct, and where the full form is given, the contracted form is often also correct.

UNIT 1 (pages 1–7)

1

2. are going to have
3. 'll be walking
4. 'll go
5. will have
6. will be walking
7. will have grown
8. will have
9. will be
10. am thinking
11. have
12. 's going to buy
13. doesn't sing
14. 's going to buy
15. are you crying

2

2. 1, 2 3. 2, 1 4. 2, 1 5. 2, 1 6. 2, 1
7. 2, 1 8. 1, 2

3

I don't think   P
I'm sending   P
you will improve   F
I haven't finished   P✔
I've written   P✔
I'm thinking   P
do you think   P
I'll also send   F
if I send   F

if they receive   F
If I post   F
I'll get   F
I probably will have
    heard   F✔
I hear   F
I'll be sitting . . .
    waiting   F
I'm counting   P

4

2. greet
3. board
4. will feel
5. venture
6. explore
7. are / have been
8. won't want
9. will have been experiencing
10. return
11. will have experienced

5

2. award
3. graduates
4. will have heard
5. will succeed
6. will be taking / will take
7. will have been operating
8. will become
9. will have gotten
10. have been going / have gone
11. will have / are going to have
12. get
13. will we all be doing
14. will have been working
15. (will have been) studying
16. will have become
17. will have

6

    have been
I ~~am~~ here in the United States for two months now, and my English is already improving. I'm writing to you in English so we can both get more practice. Classes in my intensive English program
    have been
in Chicago ~~are~~ going on for about six weeks. The
    have
instructors ~~has~~ given homework every day, and I
              am studying
have been studying a lot. In fact, I ~~study~~ right now because I have a big test tomorrow.
          learned
    Even more than in class, I have ~~learn~~ a great deal of English by talking with people in the city.
                speak
In my apartment building, most people ~~are speaking~~ English, and when I need something, I speak to the manager in English. For example, the plumbing in my apartment often doesn't work, and
I've explained
~~I'm explaining~~ the problem to the manager several times already. The plumber is coming next Tuesday, again. In fact, the same plumber
 comes
~~is coming~~ every week!
    On the negative side, the weather has been
        It's been raining / It's rained / It rains
quite bad this month. ~~It's raining~~ almost every day.
                  haven't met
In addition, sometimes I feel lonely. I ~~don't meet~~
        I haven't had / I haven't been having
many friendly people so far, and ~~I'm not having~~ any fun since I got here. So, please write to me soon! I always feel good when I hear from you.
 I'll be   *I*
~~I'm~~ very happy when ~~I'll~~ come home again
                        have
next year. When I ~~will~~ leave here, I will ~~had~~ been studying English for a year and, hopefully, will

have ~~learn~~ *learned* a lot. By this time next year I have ^ *will*

finished my studies forever, and I'll ~~work~~ *be working* with

my dad in his office. With luck I *will / am going to* learn English

well while I'm here, and that will be helpful in

Dad's business.

7

Answers will vary.

UNIT 2 (pages 8–17)

1

2. lived	8. had been growing
3. were living	9. continued
4. would	10. were benefiting
5. used to be	11. would reach
6. was	12. had reached
7. had risen	13. have lived

2

2. S, S **3.** 2, 1 **4.** 1, 2 **5.** 2, 1 **6.** S, S
7. 1, 2 **8.** 2, 1 **9.** 2, 1 **10.** 1, 2

3

2. learned	15. had been taking
3. had been working	16. got
4. came	17. would take
5. hadn't passed	18. have been having
6. was studying	19. got
7. worked	20. have been working
8. had passed	21. used to work
9. established	22. was working
10. retired	23. met
11. had been practicing	24. became
12. used to contribute	25. arrived
13. has been	26. hadn't expected
14. got	27. would succeed

4

2. b **3.** d **4.** d **5.** a **6.** b **7.** a **8.** c
9. b **10.** b **11.** b **12.** a

5

2. fix	8. didn't
3. is	9. making
4. call	10. has
5. hasn't	11. was going to
6. promises	12. take
7. buy	13. will

6

2. died / had died	10. sent
3. continued	11. would like
4. was attending	12. received
5. introduced	13. called
6. lost	14. invited
7. met	15. have spent
8. had begun	16. have traveled
9. would go / used to go / went	17. had enjoyed

7

Albert Einstein, one of the world's most renowned scientists, was born in Germany in 1879. It is said that he ~~wasn't talking~~ *didn't talk* until he was four years old, and that his parents and others believed that he was of average intelligence, or less. When he was in elementary school, his teachers ~~hadn't thought~~ *didn't think* he was a promising student. By the time he was eight years old, they ~~have~~ *had* already decided that he could not learn as fast as his classmates could. Furthermore, he didn't ~~had~~ *have* much interest in his classes, and he ~~will~~ *would* not give time to studying the required Latin and Greek.

The only subject that interested him was mathematics. However, even this interest caused trouble with his teachers; Einstein ~~has~~ *had* been solving mathematical problems in his own way, which was different from the way of the prescribed curriculum. His teachers ~~don't~~ *didn't* believe that his future ~~will~~ *would* be very bright.

When Einstein was sixteen, he left school. His parents ~~were moving~~ *had moved / moved* to Italy earlier, so he decided to follow them there. After he ~~is~~ *was / had been* in Italy for only a few months, he decided to enter another school, the Zurich Polytechnic, in Switzerland. When he arrived there, he encountered other problems: The teachers forced him to study the same subjects that the other students ~~study~~ *studied / were studying* at the time. Of course, he *had* already mastered the basic ^ subjects that were taught in the school, and so he quickly ~~had become~~ *became* bored and disillusioned. He ~~has~~ *had* been studying physics and other natural sciences by himself before that time, and he had always hoped to continue in his own way. After many frustrations, he finally ~~has~~ graduated from the Polytechnic just after he turned 21 years old. At that time, he began publishing his important scientific theories. At first, his theories weren't accepted, but after a while, other scientists

realized
~~were realizing~~ how brilliant they were, and Einstein received the recognition he deserved.

Einstein settled in the United States before World War II. He taught at Princeton University in New Jersey, and continued to make important contributions to science. In the town of Princeton,

used to walk / would walk
he ~~used to walking~~ around town like any ordinary citizen, and he was usually not recognized as the great man that he was.

Einstein's theories changed the ways that

thought
scientists ~~were thinking~~ about time, space, and matter. His ideas, such as the theory of relativity,

was
continue to be valid today. There ~~has been~~ no other scientist of such importance in the 20th century, and indeed, he is among the few great scientists of all time.

8

Answers will vary.

UNIT 3 (pages 18–22)

1

We <u>need</u> higher taxes in this town. Probably nobody <u>believes</u> me, but this is true. Nobody <u>wants</u> to pay more money, but everybody <u>desires</u> more services and a better quality of life. I <u>know</u> that these things are true:

1. We <u>don't have</u> enough police officers. More police officers <u>mean</u> safer streets and safer neighborhoods.
2. We <u>love</u> our children and we <u>appreciate</u> a good education for them. However, it <u>doesn't appear</u> that we are going to get the smaller classes, pre-kindergarten classes, and proper student advising that our young people <u>deserve</u>.
3. We drive on some roads that are in bad condition and are badly lighted. Please fix the roads and put up more and better lighting.

We <u>owe</u> it to ourselves and our children to maintain and improve our community. When our citizens <u>understand</u> the value of their tax contributions, they will <u>not mind</u> paying a little more now towards a better future.

2

2. knows	11. see
3. agree	12. hear
4. don't understand	13. am learning
5. don't use	14. don't have
6. need	15. appreciate
7. is ringing	16. cook
8. is calling	17. is coming
9. am having / have	18. am making
10. don't see	19. sounds

3

2. exactly	9. sad
3. beautiful	10. well
4. hard	11. tired
5. correctly	12. impatient
6. delicious	13. patiently; good
7. quickly	14. clear; clearly
8. good	

4

A: Hey, there! Come back! Don't go in the water!

B: Huh? What's the matter?

A: The beach is closed. Sharks are in the area today.

I don't see
B: Aw, I'm having fun. ~~I'm not seeing~~ any sharks!

dangerous
A: It doesn't matter. It doesn't look ~~dangerously~~ out there, but it is.

B: OK. OK. Gee—I've been surfing for years,

seen
and I've never ~~been seeing~~ a shark in this area!

safe
I feel very ~~safely~~ here.

we've had / we have   *there are*
A: Well, ~~we're having~~ reports that ~~there's~~ sharks in the water today—lots of them. They're congregating around that reef, right over there. Sharks especially like surfers, didn't you know that?

B: No way!

A: It's true.

Do you mean
B: ~~Are you meaning~~ that surfers have something special that attracts sharks?

A: Not exactly. When a shark sees a person on a surfboard—especially on a short surfboard—

thinks
he ~~is thinking~~ that it's a seal. The outline of the surfer from below the surface of the water looks like a seal.

serious
B: You sound ~~seriously~~.

A: I am serious. Listen to me.

B: I am listening. ~~I'm hearing~~ *I hear* you very ~~good~~ *well*, but I'm not sure I believe you!

A: Well, believe it. The sharks are behaving very ~~aggressive~~ *aggressively* today and I want all the swimmers and surfers to be safe. You can't be too ~~carefully~~ *careful*, you know.

5

Answers will vary.

UNIT 4 (pages 23–29)

1

I <u>do hope</u> we get to see you on our vacation next summer, but here's the thing: Sam and I can't agree on where to spend our next summer's vacation.

As usual, he wants to spend time in the wilderness, <u>but I don't</u>. He enjoys hiking in the woods and going kayaking, <u>but I don't</u>. Some people are city people. <u>I am</u>, and <u>I do like</u> to visit new cities all over the world. I like to wander along new streets and visit historic places, <u>but he doesn't</u>.

Sometimes I wonder how we got together! And how we stay together. <u>But, really, I do know that</u>. He loves the idea of family and togetherness, and <u>I do too</u>. He doesn't like to party much, and <u>neither do I</u>. I prefer cozy weekends at home, and <u>so does he</u>. I can't stay awake past 10:00 P.M. and <u>he can't either</u>. When we first met, I knew immediately that we would be together forever, and <u>so did he</u>.

So, to make a long story short: Hopefully, we will see you. It's not certain, <u>but it *is* possible</u> that we will be coming through Chicago on our way someplace. <u>We do want</u> to spend at least one day with you.

2

2. do too	**7.** doesn't
3. so do	**8.** does
4. aren't	**9.** neither do
5. don't	**10.** so can
6. can't	

3

2. did (survive)	**6.** do know
3. is	**7.** was
4. do eat	**8.** do understand
5. do (vote)	**9.** does have

4

2. h **3.** k **4.** j **5.** a **6.** i **7.** g **8.** b	
9. d **10.** l **11.** e **12.** f	

5

2. didn't you	**7.** have you
3. were you	**8.** wouldn't he
4. did he	**9.** was he
5. didn't it	**10.** do you
6. haven't you	

6

2. It isn't	**5.** I already have
3. I'm sure it will	**6.** They say it is
4. I know you can	

7

Some scientists have called Earth and Venus "twin planets" since in some ways they are the most similar of any two planets in the solar system. Relatively speaking, Earth is close to the sun, and Venus ~~does~~ *is*, too. They are similar, too, in size, mass, density, and volume. Both planets are "young" in terms of the universe: Earth formed about 4 or 5 billion years ago, and Venus ~~has~~ *did*, too. Earth's landscapes were formed by rain, water, sea, wind, earthquakes, and volcanoes; Venus's landscapes ~~have~~ *were* too. In fact, Earth's surface is still being formed by volcanoes; it is possible that Venus's ~~was~~ *is*, too, even though missions to Venus have not shown any active volcanoes.

On the other hand, there are remarkable differences between the planets. Most significantly, Earth supports life, but Venus ~~does~~ *doesn't*. First, it is too hot on Venus to support life. The average temperature on Earth is about 22°C, but on Venus it is 480°C. Second, Venus's atmosphere contains carbon dioxide, a poisonous gas; so ~~do~~ *does* Earth's atmosphere, although so far the carbon dioxide level from pollution has not reached lethal levels. Then, Earth has oceans, but Venus ~~don't~~ *doesn't*.

Strangely, Venus rotates from east to west, but the other planets ~~aren't~~ *don't*; they rotate from west to east. Furthermore, Earth completes a day in 24 hours, but Venus ~~don't~~ *doesn't*. It takes 243 Earth days for Venus to make a total rotation.

It's interesting, ~~doesn't~~ *isn't* it, that two planets so similar are also so different? You'll be able to see Venus as it crosses the face of the Sun in the next Transit of Venus, which will be in 2012. Will we be watching? I know we ~~are~~ *will*!

8

Answers will vary.

UNIT 5 (pages 30–39)

1

2. should	8. should
3. doesn't have to	9. ought to
4. should	10. were supposed to
5. don't have to	11. had to change
6. have to	12. should have
7. must	

2

2. b **3.** c **4.** c **5.** b **6.** a **7.** b **8.** b **9.** b **10.** a

3

I know we've all worked hard this year to sell our product. In spite of everyone's efforts, though, sales are down 9.2 percent for the year. We all (must / ~~ought to~~ / have got to) work harder now
1.
to make our company profitable. It's absolutely necessary, or the company can't survive. We (~~are supposed to do~~ / ~~should have done~~ / have to do)
2.
several essential things, starting right now. Actually, we (should have made / ~~must make~~ / ~~had to make~~)
3.
these changes a year ago, but unfortunately we didn't.

First, we (~~must have~~ / ~~could~~ / must) cut down
4.
on our overhead costs. Management had considered eliminating about 10 positions, but so far they (~~aren't supposed to~~ / ~~aren't allowed to~~ / haven't had to)
5.
lay off anybody. Instead, management says that we all (~~had better~~ / ~~should~~ / have to) take a
6.
mandatory 10 percent pay cut for this year. But, if sales go up, everyone will get a nice bonus, and salaries will go up 15 percent for next year.

We all (had better / have got to / ~~should have~~)
7.
cut down on expenses, or we won't make it. This means that there will be less travel, and nobody (~~is supposed to~~ / is allowed to / ~~has to~~) take family
8.

along on sales trips anymore. Lunches and dinners at company expense will be few and far between. We (~~must not~~ / don't have to / ~~aren't allowed to~~)
9.
entertain clients at meals; it's not necessary. We can transact our business in our offices or by phone, fax, and e-mail. Also, please be careful of company supplies. Try not to waste paper in the printer, and don't use the company phone to make your own long-distance phone calls. Even though we all know that we (are not to / ~~don't have to~~ / shouldn't) use the
10.
phone for personal calls, the rule has not been enforced. But it will be now.

Thank you for your understanding and cooperation. We'll meet on Monday to discuss this further and implement management's ideas.

4

2. should	11. can
3. can't	12. don't have to
4. can	13. must
5. don't have to	14. should
6. can	15. shouldn't
7. should	16. ought
8. shouldn't	17. might / could
9. must	18. must
10. ought	19. had better not

5

2. should I buy
3. could find
4. have to pay
5. Should I have bought
6. had better be
7. didn't have to bring
8. was supposed to do
9. are supposed to say
10. will have to come
11. should have brought
12. could have brought
13. could have learned
14. could have been

6

This is a true story about one of my students, Ana. I <u>can to</u> remember the first day she came *can*
to my class: She <u>couldn't</u> speak any English at all. *c*
She spoke only Spanish.

One time during the holidays between school terms, the dorms were closed, so the students *had to find*
<u>have to find</u> a place to live during the break. Ana

stayed with an American host family, and after the
might do
vacation, she asked me what she ~~might to do~~ to
thank her new friends for their hospitality. "Well,
C
you ~~could send~~ them a gift," I told her. "Or you
might / could just send
~~must just send~~ them a nice card."
would send
Ana decided that she ~~will send~~ a card. She
C
asked, "~~Am I supposed to get~~ a separate card for
each member of the family?"
don't have to do
"No, you ~~haven't to do~~ that. What you
C
~~ought to do~~ is get a nice card for the family and
write a thoughtful message inside."

"But my English is not so good," she
protested.

"OK, bring me the card and I'll help you
write your message," I offered.

Ana was extremely busy and easily
C
~~could have forgotten~~ her good intentions,
but she didn't. The next day after class, she
showed me a beautiful card. On the front of it
were the words "In sympathy." On the inside were
the words "You have my deepest sympathy. You
are in my thoughts at this time."

But, there was a big mistake! The card that
Ana had bought was a sympathy card, a card that
you send when someone has died. Ana had
confused the Spanish word "simpatico," which
translates to "nice" in English, with the English
word "sympathy," which expresses the emotions
of feeling sorry about someone's death.

When Ana realized her mistake, she had a
should have asked
good, long laugh. She said that she ~~must have asked~~
someone to help her pick out the right card. Now
does not need
Ana's English is excellent, and she ~~must not need~~
any help anymore.

7

Answers will vary.

UNIT 6 (pages 40–49)

1

2. have cheated
3. be very angry; be in jail
4. be operating well
5. speak Japanese
6. be very effective
7. want to anger the voters
8. have won a big victory
9. like skiing; have snowed recently

2

2.	c; can't	6.	a; should
3.	c; might; could	7.	a; might; might
4.	b; must	8.	b; must
5.	a; could; could		

3

2.	must	10.	must
3.	might	11.	must
4.	must	12.	might
5.	could	13.	may not
6.	must	14.	can't
7.	may	15.	must not
8.	could	16.	should
9.	must		

4

2. b 3. a 4. a 5. a 6. a 7. c 8. b
9. c 10. a

5

2. must be
3. couldn't eat
4. must be
5. might make
6. ought to be / should be
7. ought to be / should be
8. could have eaten
9. can still do
10. must be
11. should take
12. could have ordered

6

Answers will vary. Possible answers:

2. False   Georgia is only six months old. A baby
couldn't have committed a murder.
3. True   It's possible. We have no information
about how Mr. Nelson was killed. The
murderer could have used poison.
4. True   It's possible. She was envious of the
money, so she had a motive.
5. False   We have no reason to make this conclusion. She was asleep at the time.
6. True   He loved his brother, so it is very
unlikely that he killed him.
7. False   We have no information about the murder weapon. It might not have been a
gun.

8. True   This is a logical conclusion. Because she was envious of the Nelson's money, it means that they had more money than she did.

7

I guess you must not ~~be~~ be so happy over there. That's too bad. I'm going to give you a pep talk: Things have got *to* ~~get~~ better soon because it looks like, in your case, you think they can't *get* ~~getting~~ worse. Be realistic! Don't expect that things are going to be good all the time. *Could* ~~Must~~ it be that you're not trying hard enough to make friends? You have to go out and socialize with people. They might not be so friendly at first, but after you smile and are nice, everybody should *like* ~~have liked~~ you.

You think you've got problems? Last week Emilia left me, right after I got fired. That's right. I lost my job. Emilia must *have* ~~had~~ decided I wasn't going to be a good provider. I admit I *should* ~~must~~ have showed up on time every day, and I didn't, so that's probably why they fired me: because I was late to work a lot. I must have been crazy to be so lazy on that job at the software company.

Anyway, here I am—no job, no girlfriend. I'm feeling pretty down myself. Let me hear from you, friend.

8

Answers will vary.

UNIT 7 (pages 50–57)

1

object	C	life	NC
study	NC	thoughts	C
breadth	NC	language	NC
thought	NC	time	NC
endeavor	NC	space	NC
languages	C	symbols	C
dialects	C		

2

What does it take for a city to be voted the "Best City in the Americas"? It takes top scores in a poll that includes <u>ambience</u>, <u>friendliness</u>, <u>culture</u>, restaurants, <u>lodging</u>, and <u>shopping</u>. This year the city that ranked highest in all areas was Vancouver, British Columbia.

Located on the west coast of Canada, Vancouver has a wonderful climate, with mild <u>weather</u> and clean <u>air</u>. Although it is far north—at latitude 49°16'N—the winters are not cold because of the warm Pacific currents that flow by. Wherever you look in the area, you see spectacular <u>scenery</u>: The city is surrounded by mountains capped with <u>snow</u>, and you are never far from the sea.

The <u>water</u> and the nearby <u>wilderness</u> provide plenty of opportunities for outdoor <u>recreation</u>: <u>hiking</u>, <u>camping</u>, <u>skiing</u>, and all watersports. Because of the attributes of <u>nature</u>, the area attracts outdoor enthusiasts, and <u>tourism</u> is important here.

In addition, Vancouver has a large number of cultural events, especially in the fields of <u>music</u>, <u>art</u>, and <u>dance</u>. There is plenty of <u>entertainment</u>—theaters, concerts, art shows, and festivals—as well as many fine shops and restaurants.

The economy is usually strong. Vancouver is a major port, and it offers easy <u>transportation</u> to all parts of Canada. Because of its ideal location and multicultural community, Vancouver is the gateway of <u>commerce</u> to the entire Pacific Rim. Downtown Vancouver is the headquarters for many businesses in the fields of <u>forestry</u> and <u>mining</u>, as well as in <u>software</u>, <u>biotechnology</u>, and most recently, movies.

If Vancouver sounds like the perfect city for <u>livability</u>, to many of its residents it is. They take <u>pride</u> in their city. They expect thousands of visitors in 2010, when Vancouver will host the Winter Olympics.

3

2. a **3.** i **4.** d **5.** f **6.** h **7.** c **8.** g
9. b **10.** e

4

2. a game of
3. a game of
4. a glass of
5. a slice of / a piece of / a serving of
6. a serving of
7. a piece of / a slice of / a serving of
8. a slice of / a piece of / a serving of
9. a glass of
10. a piece of
11. a clap of
12. a flash of
13. a piece of
14. a period of

5

2. a partner	**8.** a compatible companion
3. integrity	**9.** warmth
4. work	**10.** a career
5. great fun	**11.** a job
6. love	**12.** A good salary
7. practicality	**13.** respect

6

B
2. cranberries	**6.** a salmon; salmon
3. beans	**7.** tomatoes
4. a pumpkin; pumpkin	**8.** wild rice
5. a turkey; turkey	**9.** peanuts

7

Spoken language *a* is fascinating thing, enabling us to communicate feelings and thoughts, to tell stories, and even to tell ~~lie~~ *lies*. Early in the history of **X** humankind, the use of symbols to transmit ~~idea~~ *ideas* took communication one step further. It was not necessary to be in the actual sight of another human being when one could send signals by ~~smokes~~ *smoke* or drums. But, how could ~~this communications~~ *this communication / these communications* be kept in any permanent form?

People began to record markings on hard surfaces like ~~clays~~ *clay*, using symbols to represent ~~peoples~~ *people*, animals, or, later, various ~~abstraction~~ *abstractions*. Over many thousands of years, the pictures developed into many different ~~alphabet~~ *alphabets*.

What would the world be like without writing and reading? How would ~~knowledges~~ *knowledge* pass from one generation to another? Though they are necessary today, writing and reading were not always two ~~skill~~ *skills* to be taken for granted. In fact, until recent years, **X** literacy has not been as widespread as it is now.

Technology is advancing the ways that ~~informations~~ *information* is sent and received. Computer literacy ~~have~~ *has* been added to reading and writing as a basic and necessary capability. Today, *a* person is able to learn anything from any part of the world, and to easily communicate with anyone on any part of *the* globe. We have come a long way from smoke signals in the universal instinct to connect.

8

Answers will vary.

UNIT 8 (pages 58–66)

1

2. a	**9.** the	**16.** —	**23.** the
3. —	**10.** the	**17.** —	**24.** a
4. a	**11.** a	**18.** a	**25.** the
5. a	**12.** the	**19.** —	**26.** a
6. a	**13.** a	**20.** a	**27.** The
7. The	**14.** a	**21.** a	**28.** the
8. —	**15.** —	**22.** —	

2

2. a	**9.** an	**16.** a	**23.** —
3. —	**10.** a	**17.** a	**24.** an
4. the	**11.** —	**18.** a	**25.** —
5. —	**12.** a	**19.** the	**26.** —
6. —	**13.** the	**20.** The	**27.** The
7. The	**14.** The	**21.** —	
8. a	**15.** —	**22.** the	

3

2. a	**10.** a	**18.** a	**26.** —
3. a	**11.** the	**19.** —	**27.** —
4. The	**12.** the	**20.** a	**28.** the
5. the	**13.** the	**21.** The	**29.** the
6. the	**14.** the	**22.** the	**30.** —
7. an	**15.** —	**23.** the	**31.** —
8. a	**16.** the	**24.** the	**32.** the
9. the	**17.** the	**25.** —	

4

2. an	**9.** —	**16.** a	**23.** —
3. the	**10.** —	**17.** the	**24.** —
4. the	**11.** The	**18.** the	**25.** —
5. an	**12.** —	**19.** a	**26.** the
6. a	**13.** The	**20.** the	**27.** the
7. The	**14.** —	**21.** a	**28.** —
8. a	**15.** the	**22.** —	

5

2. the	**7.** the	**12.** —	**17.** —
3. the	**8.** —	**13.** the	**18.** the
4. the	**9.** —	**14.** —	**19.** the
5. —	**10.** the	**15.** the	
6. the	**11.** —	**16.** —	

2. the	**10.** —	**18.** the	**26.** the
3. —	**11.** a	**19.** —	**27.** the
4. the	**12.** —	**20.** the	**28.** the
5. the	**13.** —	**21.** the	**29.** —
6. —	**14.** —	**22.** the	**30.** the
7. —	**15.** the	**23.** the	**31.** a
8. —	**16.** the	**24.** a	**32.** —
9. the	**17.** the	**25.** the	

7

Your Metropolitan Zoo needs you! Can you
adopt *an* animal? You can "adopt" an animal by
contributing money for its care. By adopting an
animal, you will help us keep *the* zoo in good
condition with ~~the~~ healthy animals, and you will
have ~~a~~ *the* satisfaction of knowing that your love
and your efforts are keeping "your" animal alive
and well.

   Needing adoption right now are two tigers,
one lion, two camels, a family of three
chimpanzees, and one gorilla. Which animal
would you like to adopt?

   Here is some information about the animals
needing adoption. Both our tigers are females; we
are hoping to obtain *a* male from Pakistan next year.
~~A~~ *The* lion, recently named Mufasa by a group of ~~the~~
schoolchildren, is three years old. Both camels
are *the* Arabian kind, with one hump, not *the* Bactrian
kind, with two humps. ~~Chimpanzees~~ *The chimpanzees* in our
zoo act just like *a* human family. They take care
of each other, laugh, and sometimes even have
~~the~~ arguments. We have only one gorilla now; he
is *the* most popular animal at *the* zoo, and also *the* most
expensive to maintain. He needs several sponsors.

He puts on ~~the~~ *a* show every afternoon by
interacting with ✗ visitors. He loves ~~an~~
applause that he gets.

   After you adopt ~~a~~ *an* animal, you will
regularly be advised of its life situation. You will
be honored at our annual spring banquet, and you
will receive free admission to ~~a~~ *the* zoo.

   Please find it in your heart to contribute
to *the* well-being of our animals.

8

Answers will vary.

UNIT 9 (pages 67–75)

1

   From November through March, <u>a lot of</u>
warmer-than-usual weather is expected in <u>much of</u>
the Northern Hemisphere, although not in <u>every</u>
area. Certain parts of Europe—especially the
British Isles and France—will be warm, but <u>some</u>
parts of North America—notably western Canada
and Alaska—will be somewhat colder. If the cold
conditions in these <u>two</u> places combine with warm
air currents from the coastal currents, there will be
<u>several</u> heavy snowstorms in <u>both</u> areas. The
northern parts of Asia will experience the usual
cold winter with <u>plenty of</u> snow.

   In western Africa, the weather will be cooler
than usual, and may produce <u>more</u> rain. If there is
<u>enough</u> precipitation in certain areas throughout
the continent, crop production could be greater
than usual. The river beds—<u>a great many</u> of which
had dried up during the recent drought—will
return to their normal state.

   In the Southern Hemisphere, a beautiful
spring and summer are predicted for <u>most of</u>
South America, and <u>few</u> severe storms are
expected to occur. We are expecting <u>no</u> notable
deviations from the normal temperatures or
precipitation around South America. Hopefully,
there will be <u>no</u> serious typhoons in the Pacific nor
<u>any</u> strong monsoons in Asia, but at this point, it
is impossible to tell. Nothing unusual is foreseen
for Australia, New Zealand, or Oceania; <u>each of</u>
these places will probably experience their normal
weather conditions.

   The Almanac will issue <u>one</u> detailed update
per week on this website. Click on the links to
<u>each</u> area for a more detailed report.

2

2. a few	**11.** a bunch of
3. a great deal of	**12.** a couple of
4. a little	**13.** most of
5. many	**14.** a lot of
6. any	**15.** a great deal of
7. a bit of	**16.** a few of
8. all	**17.** a little
9. A couple of	**18.** a couple of
10. every	

3

2. No	7. A few of
3. Both	8. many
4. One	9. much
5. All	10. a lot of
6. Two	11. any

4

2. All	10. both
3. no	11. no
4. each	12. Every
5. most	13. all
6. several	14. many
7. a great many	15. all
8. Each	16. a few
9. one	17. plenty of

5

2. paycheck	10. specialty
3. time	11. insurance
4. expertise	12. experience
5. professional advice	13. stock market
6. vacation	14. interests
7. year	15. money
8. goals	16. trust
9. professionals	

6

(**Many** / ~~Much~~ / **A lot of**) people in our
1.
town have been looking for a good Middle
Eastern restaurant. We have (**a few** / ~~a little~~ / **some**)
2.
Italian restaurants in the family style,
(**a couple of** / ~~a great deal of~~ / ~~every~~) French
3.
bistros, (**several** / **a few** / ~~a little~~) Asian restaurants,
4.
and (**one** / ~~some~~ / ~~every~~) Mexican restaurant, but
5.
we haven't had (~~no~~ / **any** / ~~each~~) good, authentic
6.
Middle Eastern restaurants—until now.

The new restaurant Sahara has excellent food
and service, along with (**some** / ~~any~~ / **a few**)
7.
exotic atmosphere: flowing red curtains,
(**plenty of** / **a great many** / ~~a great deal of~~)
8.
embroidered pillows on the floor, and
(~~a great deal of~~ / **a great many** / ~~every~~) Moroccan
9.
lamps hanging from the ceiling. As soon as we
arrived, we were seated in a roomy booth.
Almost immediately, a waiter brought

(**some**/ ~~a couple of~~ / ~~every~~) hot pita bread and
10.
(**some** / ~~one~~ / ~~any~~) olive oil to dip it in.
11.
To begin, my companion and I chose
(**two** / ~~one~~ / ~~both~~) different appetizers: She had
12.
(~~a little~~ / **some** / ~~one~~) stuffed grape leaves, and I
13.
had a plate of creamy hummus and tangy baba
ghanoush. (**Both** / ~~Two~~ / ~~A couple~~) of them were
14.
delicious. Then, our main courses: the lamb
kabob, which consists of pieces of lamb and
(**a few** / ~~a little~~ / ~~much~~) vegetables—onions,
15.
peppers, and mushrooms—which was tender and
tasty, and the chicken, which had been marinated
in a sauce made of (~~a little~~ / **some** / **several**)
16.
mysterious spices, was out of this world. We
both had a side dish consisting of yogurt with
(**lots of** / **several** / ~~much~~) vegetables cut up in it.
17.
Of course, we wanted dessert, and we chose
the baklava, a flaky pastry filled with
(**some** / ~~a little~~ / **plenty of**) pistachio nuts and
18.
covered with (**a little** / ~~a few~~ / ~~a couple of~~) honey.
19.
You'd better get to this restaurant soon.
Before long, when word gets around, there will be
a long wait to get in.

7

          much
It gives us ~~many~~ pleasure to write this letter
        some
to you. Our bank has ~~any~~ information which
will benefit you enormously. We are in possession
     deal of
of a great ~~many~~ money in an account with your
name on it!!! Yes, this is true. An unnamed person
has designated these funds for YOU!

In order to withdraw the money from the bank,
       a little / some
we need to request ~~a few~~ information from you:
1)   What is your Social Security number? We need
              each / every / any
     this in order to access ~~all~~ account of yours.
2)   What is your date of birth and where were
     you born? We need this information to
              all / any
     answer ~~every~~ questions about your identity.
3)   Please send the name of your bank and your
     account number. We need this so we can
                                      any
     transfer the money easily without ~~no~~
     problems with international banking laws.
             each / every
     Please write ~~all~~ number carefully.

4) What is the password for your bank account number? Please double-check this password, and make sure it is up-to-date. A great *many* ~~deal of~~ people have lost out on receiving their money because of incorrectly written passwords.

5) Please take these steps immediately. If the account is not settled by the last day of this month, you will not be able to receive *any* ~~some~~ money.

It has taken a while for us to find you. That's why you must respond quickly in order to meet the deadline for unclaimed funds. Do not take *much* ~~many~~ time to respond or you will lose *all* ~~each~~ of the money in your account!

Also, very important! Please keep this matter confidential. Even if only a *few* ~~little~~ people find out about this, it could make *much / a lot of* ~~many~~ trouble with the bureaucracy.

8

Answers will vary.

UNIT 10 (pages 76–83)

1

2. bright young
3. new spring
4. various international
5. exciting big
6. long, straight
7. smallest added
8. expensive silk
9. old Japanese
10. beautiful classic
11. elegant business
12. fabulous, modern
13. wild, brightly colored
14. tropical South Sea
15. casual summer
16. liveliest new
17. hot pink
18. brilliant purple
19. long cotton
20. well-known contemporary
21. fabulous new

2

2. flower gardens
3. vegetable gardens
4. work horses
5. show horses
6. house cats
7. family dogs
8. dog house
9. strawberry jam
10. blackberry tea
11. peach pie
12. kitchen table
13. childhood memories
14. childhood dreams
15. baby sister
16. summer night

3

2. 1 two-hundred-year-old dining room table
3. 8 velvet-covered dining room chairs
4. 2 century-old Tiffany lamps
5. 1 silver-plated samovar
6. 2 (one) hundred-(and)-fifty-year-old rocking chairs
7. 1 hand-woven Persian carpet
8. 1 hand-written manuscript
9. 3 ivory-inlaid coffee tables
10. 4 hand-painted serving dishes
11. 2 hand-carved mahogany beds
12. 2 (one) hundred-(and)-thirty-year-old, gold-inlaid vases

4

2. local coffee shop
3. student ethics council
4. international student activities
5. old, dilapidated houses / dilapidated old houses
6. attention deficit disorder
7. Four-Year Service Award
8. Five-State Volunteerism Award

5

Moving from the *fresh country* ~~country fresh~~ air to the head-clogging, polluted stuff that city dwellers breathe presents a shock to the body. Ten years ago, I had miraculously obtained a well-paying job in the *glamorous publishing* ~~publishing glamorous~~ world, and I moved with my wife and two daughters from *beautiful southwest* ~~southwest beautiful~~ Montana with its *clear blue* ~~blue clear~~ skies to New York, where there appeared to us to be no skies at all, only *dirty gray* ~~gray dirty~~ smog.

Within a week, my wife and children and I all came down with a *mysterious respiratory* ~~respiratory mysterious~~ ailment. Coughing and sneezing, with eyes and noses dripping, we suffered for 10 days. A *10-day* ~~10-days~~ siege in a small four-room apartment felt like being imprisoned in a *cold, cement* ~~cement, cold~~ jail cell. We were accustomed to being outdoors, in the open Montana air. After only two weeks at my *prized new* ~~new prized~~ job, I had to call in sick. And was I

sick! My ~~42 years old feverish~~ *feverish 42-year-old* [two mistakes]
body ached as it never had ached before.
~~Iron gigantic~~ *Gigantic iron* hammers pounded in my head. My
lungs felt like ~~lead huge~~ *huge lead* weights. I coughed
constantly, so that I never had more than a
~~two hours~~ *two-hour* rest, even though I took double the
recommended dose of the ~~cough over the counter~~ *over-the-counter cough*
medicine we had bought at the ~~drug corner~~ *corner drug* store.
Finally, after 10 days, we recovered physically,
although not psychologically, from our
~~New York rude~~ *rude New York* reception. My first three weeks
in the Big Apple gave me the feeling that I lived in
a foreign and hostile country—and it took many
months until I felt differently. Now I love New
York, I love to breathe the ~~New York wonderful~~ *wonderful New York*
air, and you couldn't get me to live anyplace else.

6

Answers will vary.

UNIT 11 (pages 84–93)

1

This is the story of a very simple invention
<u>that you can find in almost every office in the
whole world today</u>. It is also the story of an
inventor <u>whose creativity and persistence resulted
in a very useful product</u>. What is the famous
invention? It is Liquid Paper, the white liquid <u>that
covers up the mistakes you make when writing or
typing</u>. It was invented in the early 1950s by Bette
Nesmith Graham, a secretary in Dallas, Texas,
<u>who began using tempera paint to cover up the
typing errors in her work</u>.

At the time, Ms. Nesmith was a 27-year-old
single mother of one son, struggling to make ends
meet and working as a secretary to the chairman
of a big Dallas bank. When she began to work
with her first electric typewriter, she found that the
type marks <u>she typed onto the paper</u> didn't erase
as cleanly as those from manual typewriters. So
Ms. Nesmith, <u>who was also an artist</u>, quietly
began painting out her mistakes. Soon she was
supplying bottles of her homemade preparation,
<u>which she called Mistake Out</u>, to other secretaries
in the building.

When she lost her job with the company, Ms.
Nesmith turned to working full time to develop
the Mistake Out as a business, expanding from

her house into a small trailer <u>she had bought for
the backyard</u>. In hopes of marketing her product,
she approached IBM, <u>which turned her down</u>. She
stepped up her own marketing and within a
decade was a financial success. The product,
<u>which came to be called Liquid Paper</u>, was
manufactured in four countries and sold in nearly
three dozen. In fiscal 1979, <u>which ended about six
months before she sold the company</u>, it had sales
of $38 million, <u>of which $3.5 million was net
income</u>. By the time <u>Ms. Nesmith finally sold her
business to Gillette in 1979</u>, she had built her
simple, practical idea into a $47.5 million
business.

It is heartwarming that the story has a happy
ending in more ways than one. Ms. Nesmith
remarried and became Mrs. Graham. Her son,
Michael, a musician <u>of whom she was
understandably proud</u>, became very successful as
one of a music group called the Monkees, <u>which
appeared on an NBC television show for several
years in the mid-1960s</u>. Subsequently a country-
rock musician, a songwriter, and a video producer,
he now heads a production company in California,
<u>where he also directs some charities</u>.

With some of her profits, Mrs. Graham
established a foundation <u>whose purpose is to
provide leading intellectuals with the time, space,
and compatible colleagues</u> <u>that they need to
ponder and articulate the most important social
problems of our era</u> [two clauses]. Bette Nesmith
Graham first developed a product <u>that there was
clearly a need for</u>; then she used the substantial
profits for charitable purposes, <u>which is a fine
thing to do</u>.

The story of Liquid Paper and Bette Nesmith
Graham is a story <u>everyone can appreciate</u>. It
shows how a wonderful product came to market
because of the cleverness and perseverance of its
inventor. Perhaps you, too, have a clever idea <u>that
will spread like wildfire</u> if only you can give it the
kind of spark <u>that Mrs. Graham gave to her
product</u>.

2

2. whom	9. which
3. who	10. which
4. whom	11. when
5. where	12. which
6. which	13. that
7. who	14. that
8. —	15. whose

3

2. which	4. whose
3. who	5. which

6. who
7. whose
8. who
9. who
10. who
11. when

12. who
13. who
14. whose
15. who
16. that
17. whom

4

2. which
3. where
4. who / that
5. which / that
6. who / whom / that / —
7. which / that / —
8. which / that / —
9. that / which / —

10. whose
11. who / that
12. when / that
13. which / that
14. which / that
15. which / that
16. which / that / —

5

2. who / that feels energized around others
3. whose energies are activated by being alone
4. who / that pay attention to details in the world
5. who / that is more interested in relationships between people and things
6. that / which / 0 this test measures
7. who / that made decisions objectively
8. whose primary way to reach a conclusion was (this:)
9. who / that took other people's feelings into consideration
10. that/which / 0 he or she has
11. which we prefer to live or work
12. who / that prefer a planned and predictable environment
13. that / which / 0 they find themselves in OR in which they find themselves
14. whose life must be planned in advance
15. where he should be placed to most enhance the company OR
in which he should be placed to most enhance the company OR
that / which / 0 he should be placed in to most enhance the company
16. which you would be the happiest and most productive

6

2. A 3. A 4. A 5. B 6. B
7. A 8. A 9. B 10. B

7

One of the ways in ~~when~~ *which* people can be classified is by labeling them *extroverts* and *introverts*. However, there are other methods,

some of ~~them~~ *which* are now considered to have little scientific value, that people use to conveniently categorize members of the human race.

For example, there is the division into mesomorphs, who are muscular; endomorphs, who tend to be fat; and ectomorphs, who are thin. The endomorph is stereotyped as a relaxed person without obsessions, whereas the ectomorph is stereotyped as a person ~~whom~~ *who* is nervous and serious and who rarely smiles.

Another easily made division defines people as Type A and Type B. Type A is the category to ~~whom~~ *which* people belong if they are very serious, ambitious, and driven. Type A originally described people, usually middle-aged males, ~~whom~~ *who* suffered a lot of heart attacks. Type B, on the other hand, labels a rather passive, ambitionless person of ~~that~~ *whom* others frequently take advantage, and ~~which~~ *who* is probably not a candidate for a heart attack.

Some people categorize human beings by the astrological sign that they were born under ⱑ. For example, a person who *was* born between April 22 and May 21 is called a Taurus and is supposed to possess certain characteristics, such as congeniality and tact. A person that *was* born between June 22 and July 21 is a Cancer and is reputed to be stubborn but effective. There are 12 such categories, which encompass all the months of the year. Many people base their lives and relationships on the predictions ~~what~~ *which / that* are made by astrologers.

One recent theory to categorize people is the theory of left-brained and right-brained people. According to this theory, right-brained people, ~~that~~ *who* are intuitive and romantic, are the artists and creative people of the world. Left-brained people, who ~~they~~ are logical in their thinking, turn out to be mathematicians and scientists. According to this theory, people whose ~~their~~ abilities are not developed enough in certain areas can develop the side of the brain they want to improve ⱑ in order to better balance their personality.

All of these theories, which in themselves are too simplistic, are indeed unscientific. However, they have provided attractive and sometimes amusing solutions for people *who* are looking for easy ways to understand the human race. Different theories of categorizing people, which ⱑ is always a difficult thing to do, will continue to come and go.

Answers will vary.

UNIT 12 (pages 94–101)

1

Carolina Manning, daughter of Dr. and Mrs. John Manning of Boston, was married on Sunday to Matthias Wolfe, the son of Dr. Maria and Mr. Douglas Wolfe of New York. Reverend Harry Carter performed the ceremony at the All-Faiths Religious Center in Boston.

Ms. Manning will continue to use her name professionally. She is well-known as the originator of the children's television show *Hot Ice Cream*, of which she is both the writer and producer. She has a degree in film studies from the University of Southern California and she also received a master's degree in cinematography from New York University. Her father, whose text on Shakespeare is required reading in many colleges, is a professor of English at Boston University, at which he holds the John B. Baker Chair of English Literature. Her mother taught in the public school system for 30 years, the last 20 of which were at Grisham High School, where she was principal. She retired last June.

Mr. Wolfe is a law clerk in the office of Superior Court Judge Ruth Heller, for whom he had worked during the two previous summers. He has a degree in Public Administration from Syracuse University, from which he graduated magna cum laude, and a law degree from Boston University. His father is an editor at Koala Publications, a children's book publisher. His mother, Dr. Maria Lopez Manning, is a pediatrician currently serving as Chief of Pediatrics at Children's Hospital.

The bride and bridegroom met at the Woodland Fire Department last November, while waiting in a long line to vote. They soon discovered that they had common values, many of which are political. Ms. Manning is active in the Southside Independent Voters Caucus, dedicated to informing citizens about current issues. Mr. Wolfe occasionally publishes his letters of opinion, some of which have drawn national attention, in the Beacon Globe.

Ms. Manning will be known socially as Mrs. Wolfe. The couple, several of whose friends and colleagues live in the same wooded complex, will reside in Contemplation Woods, near the fire department at which they first met.

2

2. True; one of which was done recently; almost all of whom suffered
3. False; most of which are available
4. False; the majority of whom were physically fit
5. False; most of whom do not have
6. True; all of which are absorbed; many of whom have
7. False; most of which are; all of which are labeled
8. False; the amount of which doesn't change

3

2. looking for his missing son
3. transformed by a magic spell
4. brilliantly portrayed by Tom Cruise
5. adapted from the TV series
6. turned into a nightmare
7. zipping him from Amsterdam to Las Vegas
8. starring Leonardo DiCaprio and Kate Winslet
9. capable of a power that may destroy him
10. Francis Ford Coppola's Oscar-winning version

4

Additional answers may be possible.

2. Cinema pubs contain independent sections of tables and comfortable swivel chairs, allowing you to feel like you are in your own living room.
3. Servers, most of whom are local college students, come to each table before the movie begins and take orders for food and beverages.
4. The ambience in the theater is similar to that in a cabaret, where there is an intimate feeling.
5. In accordance with the cozy atmosphere, the cinema pubs show small films, many of which are from other countries.
6. Although you have come to the theater to see a movie, you will also find that the cinema pub is a gathering place where people like to socialize.
7. The idea of the cinema pub, already popular in the United Kingdom, is beginning to catch on in the United States.
8. Cinema pubs show recent films in a relaxed atmosphere, making them a welcome alternative to huge and impersonal movie multiplexes.
9. For a change of pace, see your next film at the cinema pub nearest to you.

5

After World War II, Europe was the center of important developments in filmmaking, which ~~they~~ strongly influenced motion pictures worldwide. In Italy, well-known movies, some of ~~them~~ *which* were Rossellini's *Open City,* ~~making~~ *made* in 1945, and De Sica's *Shoeshine* (1946) and *Bicycle Thief* (1948), established a trend toward realism in film. These directors weren't concerned with contrived plots or stories ~~that~~ produced for entertainment value alone; they took their cameras into the streets to make films ~~showed~~ *showing* the harshness of life in the years after the war.

In the next decades, Federico Fellini—~~was~~ an outstanding director—combined realistic plots with poetic imagery, symbolism, and philosophical ideas in now-classic films, the most famous of ~~them~~ *which* is *La Strada,* ~~which~~ a movie ostensibly about circus people in the streets but really about the meaning of life.

In France, a group of young filmmakers, ~~calling~~ *called* the "New Wave," appeared during the 1950s. This group developed a new kind of focus, which stressed characterization rather than plot and featured new camera and acting techniques, ~~seeing~~ *seen* in movies such as Truffaut's *400 Blows*.

In England, another group of filmmakers, ~~was~~ known as the "Angry Young Man" movement, developed a new realism. In Sweden, Ingmar Bergman used simple stories and allegories to look at complex philosophical and social issues, some of ~~them~~ *which* are masterfully explored in *The Seventh Seal*. The Spaniard Luis Buñuel depicted social injustices and used surrealistic techniques, creating films like *Viridiana*.

Postwar developments in filmmaking were not limited to Western Europe. The Japanese director Akira Kurosawa, ~~was~~ the first Asian filmmaker to have a significant influence in Europe, made *Rashomon* in 1950. Movies from India, like Satyajit Ray's *Pather Panchali,* showed us life on the subcontinent. Even in Russia, where filmmaking was under state control, it was possible to make movies like *The Cranes Are Flying,* ~~portray~~ *portraying* the problems of the individual. Russian directors also made films based on literary classics, ~~included~~ *including* Shakespeare's plays and Tolstoy's monumental historical novel, *War and Peace*.

In summary, in the decades after World War II, filmmaking turned in new directions, as shown by a wide range of movies from around the world, many of them focused on the meaning of life and how to interpret it.

6

Answers will vary.

UNIT 13 (pages 102–111)

Storyville School Vandalized
STORYVILLE—Storyville's Country Day School <u>was vandalized</u> last weekend. Some of the items that <u>were stolen</u> from the school were five computers, a CD player, and sports equipment, the value of which is approximately $11,000. No clues <u>were left</u> by the thieves, and as of this morning, information as to their identity <u>was still being sought</u> by police. School officials <u>could not be contacted</u> for comment.

Restaurant Burglarized After Hours
MARGARITAVILLE—The Margaritaville Cantina <u>was burglarized</u> just before dawn on Sunday morning. Police found that the lock on the back door <u>had been altered</u> prior to the burglary. This is the third time since November that restaurants in the 3400 block of Aspen Avenue <u>have been broken into</u>. Police Chief Bill Griffin stated that a full investigation <u>is being made</u> and that he expects that the perpetrators <u>will be arrested</u> shortly. The owner of the restaurant states that he is <u>going to have a better alarm system installed</u>.

Barking Dog Removed to Shelter
WESTVIEW—A barking dog that belongs to a family in the 400 block of Pear Tree Street is the source of problems between neighbors. Sunday afternoon a complaint <u>was filed</u> with police by next-door neighbors, who claim that their peace <u>is always being disturbed</u> by the dog's constant barking. They state that they <u>should not be forced</u> to endure the noise, and they want to <u>have the dog removed</u> from the property. The owners are out of town and <u>cannot be reached</u>. The dog <u>is being cared for</u> temporarily at the City Animal Shelter.

Cash Register Damaged, Waiter Is Fired
NORTHSIDE—An upset waiter at Pop's Place smashed the computer screen of a restaurant cash register after midnight on Wednesday. The waiter, 22, <u>was fired</u> but <u>was not arrested</u>. His manager wanted <u>to have the incident documented</u> by police

and <u>to have the alleged offender barred</u> from the premises in the future. The damage <u>is estimated</u> at $1,100.

2

2. will be caressed
3. laze
4. savor
5. will be thrilled
6. must be visited
7. must be enjoyed
8. are spoken
9. will be amazed
10. was settled
11. were enchanted
12. left
13. can experience
14. speak
15. will be delighted
16. was colonized
17. is considered
18. are not allowed
19. may be rented
20. are imported / have been imported

3

2. would actually be employed
3. is sustained
4. were sent
5. are maintained
6. must be controlled
7. cannot be grown
8. is obscured
9. has to be done
10. is produced
11. is recycled
12. is used
13. have been utilized
14. were developed
15. am known
16. are made
17. can be found
18. have it collected
19. is filtered
20. is being built
21. will be completed

4

A Underlined Causatives:

1. having their apartment sprayed
2. had some furniture sent
3. have it shortened; have future alterations done
4. have had it checked
5. had had a car sent

B New Causatives:

2. have your table looked at by an insurance adjuster
3. have the bill sent to him
4. can get the problem fixed
5. have your son picked up

5

2. get my car fixed
3. got towed
4. got charged
5. got stolen
6. got dumped
7. get hired
8. gets asked
9. get fired

6

1. b. They can be toasted easily.
   c. They were introduced to Mexico by the Spanish.
   d. And before that, they had been brought to Spain by the Moors.
2. a. Pepitas are eaten whole.
   b. They also are ground for use in sauces.
   c. Even if the pepitas have been ground, the sauce has a rough texture.
   d. Pepitas have been used since pre-Colombian times.
3. a. In Mexico, it is made of unsmoked meat and spices.
   b. In Spain, the meat is smoked.
4. a. In Mexico, jicama is sold by street vendors.
   b. It is eaten in thick slices that have been sprinkled with salt, lime juice, and chili powder.
5. a. Avocados are considered a true delicacy.
   b. If they are hard, they should be allowed to ripen.
   c. Guacamole is made from avocados.
   d. Avocados also are used in salads and as a garnish.
6. a. Meat is steamed in little packets of banana leaves.
   b. First, the leaves must be softened over a flame.
   c. Then, the meat and other ingredients are wrapped in them.
7. a. They are cooked in various ways, including deep-frying and baking.
   b. Firm green bananas may be substituted.
8. a. They can be eaten with any meal.
   b. They are made from corn or wheat flour.
   c. Tortillas can now be found in supermarkets.
9. a. Chilies are used to season many different dishes.
   b. Chili-seasoned foods have been consumed for more than 8,000 years.

10. **a.** Corn is used widely in Mexico.
    b. In Mexican cooking, no part of the corn is wasted.
    c. The ears, husks, silk, and kernels are used in different ways.
    d. This was the first plant that was cultivated in Mexico.

7

I could tell you many things about radium and radioactivity and how they were ~~discovering~~ *discovered*, but it would take a long time. Since we have only a short time, I'll give you a short account of my early work with radium. The conditions of the discovery were peculiar, and I am always ~~pleasing~~ *pleased* to remember them and to explain them.

In the year 1897, my husband, Professor Curie, and I ~~were worked~~ *were working / worked* in the laboratory of the school of Physics and Chemistry, where he held his lectures. I was ~~engage~~ *engaged* in work on uranium rays, which had *been* discovered two years before by Professor Becquerel.

In my research, I found out that uranium and thorium compounds were active in proportion to the amount of uranium or thorium that they ~~got~~ contained; in other words, the more uranium or thorium ~~that contained~~ *that was contained / contained / Ø* in the compound, the greater the activity.

Then I thought that some unknown element must ~~be existed~~ *exist* among those minerals, one with a much greater radioactivity than uranium or thorium. And I thought that it should be found. I wanted to find and to separate that element, so I went to work on that with Professor Curie. We thought we would have the project ~~doing~~ *done* in several weeks or months, but it was not so. It took many years of hard work to finish that task. There was not one new element that we found—there were several. But the most important was radium.

Now, if we take a practical point of view, then the most important property of the rays is the way they influence the cells of the human organism. These effects may ~~use~~ *be used* for the cure of several diseases. Good results have ~~be~~ *been* obtained in many cases. What is considered particularly important is the treatment of cancer.

But, we must not forget that when radium *was* discovered, no one knew that it would prove useful in hospitals. The work was one of pure science. And this is a proof that scientific work must ~~be not~~ *not be* considered from the point of view of its direct usefulness. It must be ~~doing~~ *done* for itself, for the beauty of science.

There is always a vast field which is left to experimentation, and I hope that we may have some beautiful progress in the following years. It is my earnest desire that this scientific work should *be* carried on, hopefully by some of you, and that it will be ~~appreciating~~ *appreciated* by all of you, who understand the beauty of science.

8

Answers will vary.

UNIT 14 (pages 112–116)

1

Good evening ladies and gentlemen! It is being reported at this moment that smoke signals have been spotted on Pirates' Island, which is located about seven miles from where the sailboat *Belle* was last seen yesterday. It is believed that these smoke signals are being made by survivors of the *Belle,* which must have sunk or been blown ashore during a sudden squall. Navy helicopters are speeding out to the island at this moment.

The sailboat is owned by the Crane family, and it is thought that the whole family—Pat, Jesse, their 12-year-old son and their 10-year-old daughter—was aboard, as well as another family who is related to them—cousins from Canada, it was said.

The area where the Cranes were sailing is rocky and it is considered dangerous; however, the Cranes are known to be excellent sailors and could have avoided the dangerous rocks under normal circumstances. But the squall that came up was said to have near-hurricane-force winds.

Oh, this just in! One Navy helicopter is landing. The pilot is reporting that he sees seven people waving at the plane. So, this is good news, viewers. The survivors are assumed to be all right. Stay tuned to this channel for more news after this message . . .

2

2. is believed
3. was previously thought

4. is understood
5. is well known
6. would be perceived
7. is widely confirmed
8. has been well established
9. are known
10. has been considered
11. can be asssumed

3

2. is believed	8. is claimed
3. is said	9. is known
4. is not known	10. was conjectured
5. is now assumed	11. is known
6. is also thought	12. is thought
7. are now believed	13. can safely be assumed

4

      is
It often said that a full moon causes many
  ^
bad things to happen. More crimes, disasters, and
  are
accidents alleged to occur during the times when
      ^
the moon is full, so many people take extra care
during these times. People have been known to
plan their lives around the phrases of the moon;
     it
for example, is believed by some that the phase of
      ^
the moon determines when is the best time to buy
or sell stocks and other investments.

    These beliefs about a full moon, however,
have been shown to have no basis in fact,
according to many scientists. Numerous studies
       conducted
have been ~~conducting~~, and no relationship
between a full moon and higher rates of anything
has been proven. This includes the homicide rate,
traffic accidents, crisis calls to police or fire
stations, births of babies, major disasters, casino
payout rates, assassinations, aggression by
professional hockey players, psychiatric
admissions, emergency room admissions,
sleepwalking, or any other of a myriad of
         believed   *regulated*
happenings that are often ~~believe~~ to be ~~regulating~~
by the moon.

    If a significant correlation between the full
moon and these occurrences has not been shown,
           assumed
why are these so-called lunar myths ~~assuming~~ to
be true by so many? Sociologists say that the bases
       found
of many lunar myths are ~~finding~~ in folklore. For
     has
example, it ~~have~~ been believed since ancient times
that more births occur during a full moon and

          committed
more crimes are ~~committing~~ during a full moon,
even though these ideas are not verified by
statistics. Beliefs like these are advanced by the
effect of today's media; lunar myths are frequently
presented in films and works of fiction. It makes a
         seen
good story when events are ~~seeing~~ as being
controlled by the moon.

    There are also some misconceptions that
contribute to the idea that the moon has a
powerful effect on the human body and therefore
                         is
behavior is affected by it. For instance, it claimed
                         ^
by many that the earth and the human body both
  composed
are ~~composing~~ of 80 percent water, and that the
moon thus influences the body just as it does the
earth's tides. But this is not entirely true. Eighty
percent of the *surface* of the earth is water.
Furthermore, only *unbounded* bodies of water—
                affected
such as oceans and seas—are ~~affect~~ by the moon,
but the water in the human body is bounded.
Even though the powers of the moon have been
discredited by some scientific research, the
     is
moon still considered a strong, indefinable symbol
     ^
of romance and mystery throughout the world.

5

Answers will vary.

UNIT 15 (pages 117–126)

1

    Thank you for <u>writing</u> to Zenith University.
You have asked what qualities are necessary for
<u>gaining</u> admittance to the freshman class.

    Zenith University seeks to attract
academically talented students who will have the
greatest possibility of <u>succeeding</u> and <u>thriving</u> here,
and who will also participate in <u>contributing</u> to
the growth of the University community. The most
important factors are:

- <u>Completing</u> high school with a grade point
  average (GPA) of 3.5 or higher
- <u>Achieving</u> a score of 1875 or higher on the
  standardized Scholastic Aptitude Test (SAT)
- <u>Being</u> recommended by high school teachers
  and counselors
- <u>Demonstrating</u> evidence of <u>being involved</u>
  in the world

In addition to GPA, the Board considers the
overall level of achievement, enrollment in honors
courses, individual academic strengths, and class

rank. For example, you must be in the top quarter of your high school class, and the higher your rank, the greater your chance of <u>becoming</u> part of our student body. Of course, <u>receiving</u> good recommendations from teachers and counselors also tells us that you will be able to succeed in your academic work here.

 <u>Taking</u> interest in the world is shown by your <u>having</u> participated in extra-curricular activities in high school, such as <u>playing</u> sports, <u>writing</u> for the school newspaper, and <u>taking part</u> in student government. Involvement is also evidenced by your <u>showing</u> concern for your community, as demonstrated by activities such as <u>volunteering</u> in hospitals and <u>being</u> active in political campaigns. <u>Displaying</u> an interest in other cultures is also desirable, and the university looks favorably upon candidates who have spent time <u>studying</u> or <u>traveling</u> abroad.

 Along with your application, you will send a personal essay. The importance of <u>writing</u> this essay is significant, because it demonstrates your <u>thinking</u> skills and your abilities in <u>expressing</u> yourself. The Board of Admissions carefully reviews every application for undergraduate admission in <u>deciding</u> whom to admit.

 We wish you good luck in your application process.

2

2. h   **3.** g   **4.** a   **5.** c   **6.** d   **7.** b   **8.** e

3

2. carving	**7.** taking
3. Playing	**8.** Collecting
4. Knitting	**9.** keeping
5. Traveling	**10.** riding
6. telling	**11.** reading

4

2. not having been	**6.** having telephoned
3. having stopped by	**7.** having become
4. having seen	**8.** not having stopped
5. having met	

5

2. having been employed / being employed
3. being hung up on
4. being interrupted
5. being bothered
6. being left alone
7. being bombarded
8. being trapped
9. not being disturbed
10. not being telephoned

11. being intruded upon
12. being solicited
13. Being required
14. having been interrupted
15. being concerned
16. having been annoyed

6

2. Her finding
3. Mary's working
4. George's having come / George's coming
5. Henry's constant fiddling
6. Nicole's falling down
7. her constant complaining
8. Jim's leaving
9. his coming

7

On February 28, 2004, Keizo Miura celebrated his birthday by ~~ski~~ *skiing* down a two-mile run at a Rocky Mountain ski resort. A man's skiing two miles down a mountain run is not usually worthy of being noticed, but in this case it is—his birthday was his hundredth birthday.

 Miura celebrated his 100th year by ~~descend~~ *descending* the mountain together with more than 120 friends and family members from Japan, all regular and robust skiers. After the descent, Miura said: "There is no better way to celebrate my 100th birthday than being able to wholeheartedly enjoy ~~ski~~ *skiing* with my family and friends."

 ~~Him~~ *His* succeeding in this descent was just one more of his many accomplishments. The year before, for his 99th birthday, Miura had skied down Mont Blanc in the French Alps. Every year for the six months from November to May, he spends the time ~~to ski~~ *skiing* in Japan and abroad.

 Miura might not have embraced the sport without ~~have~~ *having* worked at the Aomori Forestry Bureau; it was there that his strong interest in skiing developed. After Miura retired, he continued ~~poured~~ *pouring* his energies into the sport, not only by ~~ski~~ *skiing* frequently, but also by ~~to work~~ *working* on the technical committee for the Ski Association of Japan. His son Yuchiro Miura is a champion skier too, no doubt because of having been ~~inspiring~~ *inspired* by his father. The younger Miura became the oldest man—at age 71—to reach the summit of Mount Everest. Mountain climbing is another of Keizo

Miura's activities as well—at 77, he himself
succeeded in ~~climb~~ *climbing* Mount Kilimanjaro, the tallest
mountain in Africa.

To what does Miura credit his having stayed
in shape for all these years? One thing is eating
well. Decades ago, he began training, and he
~~adapting~~ *adapted* his diet so that he could ski after ~~turned~~ *turning*
50. He eats nutritious food, such as unpolished
rice, fish, seaweed, and soybeans. Another thing is
exercising regularly. Every morning he goes
through a routine of ~~move~~ *moving* his neck left and right
100 times, ~~open~~ *opening* his mouth wide, and ~~stick~~ *sticking* out his
tongue. He says this prevents the area around his
mouth from ~~be~~ wrinkling. He also does squats and
other exercises ~~for to strengthen~~ *for strengthening / to strengthen* the body, and he
walks 3–4 kilometers each day.

Miura has benefited enormously from having
~~been~~ eaten healthfully and having ~~exercising~~ *exercised*
religiously for the past half-century. "I still feel
good," he says. "It's about diet, it's about exercise.
. . . It's about making the most out of a long life."

8 _____

Answers will vary.

UNIT 16 (pages 127–135)

1 _____

Human beings need <u>to be loved and cared for</u>.
When warm feelings exist between people, it is
natural <u>to give</u> and <u>to accept</u> love. In fact, a
common proverb is: "It is better <u>to give</u> than <u>to
receive</u>."

Children who do well in school seem <u>to be
receiving</u> strong and consistent love and support
from their families. On the other hand, many
antisocial adolescents appear <u>not to have been
given</u> much tender, loving care during their
childhood. In their desire <u>to be included</u> in a
group, some teenagers are easily seduced into
gangs. Often they are disappointed <u>not to receive</u>
from other gang members the love that they had
been yearning for.

After spending years in a gang, it is common
for these young people <u>to become hardened</u>; it is
then extremely difficult for them <u>to re-enter</u> society.
Unfortunately, most are expected <u>to continue</u> on
their sad and seemingly hopeless journey through
life. However, some who are fortunate enough
<u>to have been reached and touched</u> by enlightened
and caring social workers do reform and become

productive members of society. With guidance and
help, it is possible, even for those exhibiting
antisocial behaviors, <u>to be rehabilitated</u>.

The purpose of this paper is <u>to identify</u>
agencies and facilities in this state which have
done significant work in rehabilitating troubled
youngsters, and <u>to outline</u> their programs of
treatment. In the final section of the paper, I
attempt <u>to evaluate</u> these programs.

2 _____

2. to celebrate
3. to spend
4. to sing
5. to enjoy
6. to see
7. to be included / to have been included
8. to know
9. to be given
10. to have been remembered / to be remembered
11. to joke
12. to tell
13. to be teased

3 _____

2. (d) I would go to the Caribbean (in order) to
sail, swim, dive, and snorkel.
3. (f) I would go to Switzerland or Colorado (in
order) to ski.
4. (e) I would go to Egypt (in order) to visit the
pyramids.
5. (i) I would go to Japan (in order) to see
Mount Fuji.
6. (a) I would go to Kenya (in order) to photo-
graph large wild animals.
7. (b) I would go to Paris (in order) to shop for
original designer clothes.
8. (j) I would go to Italy (in order) to walk
around the ruins of ancient Rome.
9. (c) I would go to Brazil (in order) to dance the
samba and bossa nova.
10. (g) I would go to Disneyland (in order) to
meet Mickey Mouse and Donald Duck.

4 _____

2. to dance
3. to be
4. to have been
5. to be remembered / to have been remembered
6. to reminisce
7. to cry
8. to hide
9. to love
10. (to) cherish
11. to attend

5

2. to love	13. (to) try
3. to be	14. to go
4. to be picked up	15. to be attacked
5. (to be) given	16. to walk
6. to ride	17. to go
7. to be invited	18. to drive
8. to visit	19. to let / to have let
9. to make	20. to have been
10. to talk	21. To lose / To have lost
11. to tell	22. to have had
12. (to) imagine	

6

2. to learn
3. to work
4. to do
5. to get
6. To be
7. to show up
8. to take
9. to leave
10. to allow
11. to give
12. to have gotten
13. to be given / to have been given
14. to be taken advantage of
15. to invest
16. to have been tricked
17. to tell
18. to forget
19. to pursue
20. to be
21. to talk
22. to be told
23. To get
24. to behave
25. to go out

7

    "To be or not ^to^ be"—this is a famous quotation from Shakespeare's *Hamlet*. The quotation is relevant to me because for the past two years I have been thinking about what I am and what I want ~~being~~ ^to be^.

    In spite of having quite an average upbringing, I was different from my friends because I preferred ~~to not~~ ^not to^ watch TV, but to read. Not that I didn't participate in childhood games and high school sports—I was involved like most young people, and my parents encouraged ^me^ to take part in several

activities. But, I also chose to ~~reading~~ ^read^ for a few hours each day, or more likely, each night. Sometimes I didn't even stop ~~going~~ ^to go^ to sleep. As a child, I read the usual children's books, but I soon attempted to read newspaper articles and magazines about science, and a few years later, about philosophy. Since I had learned to read without difficulty at age three, it was easy enough for me ~~stepping~~ ^to step^ up to a higher level.

    Because of my interests in science and philosophy, I have always tended to balance the one area with the other in my mind. The result of spending so much time reading and trying to integrate everything I was absorbing was that I became quite a reflective person. I didn't appear ~~being~~ ^to be^ a "geek" or even an intellectual kid; I seemed ~~acted~~ ^to act^ like everybody else. And, in truth, I was like everyone else, except that I also had a more introspective side than most kids.

    This description of myself is meant to show that I have been thinking about myself and what I wish ~~becoming~~ ^to become^. The truth is that I do not know yet; it is too soon ^to^ know. This is why I hope to attend Zenith University—^to^ get a broad exposure to all the humanities and sciences and find the field where I will be able ^to^ maximize my abilities and find fulfillment. At the moment, I think I would like ^to^ be an archeologist and do research about the beliefs and religious practices of ancient peoples. But, I will seek to expose myself to many disciplines at Zenith, and to benefit from learning about all of them.

    In Zenith's motto, the words—"To learn is to grow"—are meant for me. That is what I expect ^to^ do and will endeavor to ~~doing~~ ^do^ at Zenith University.

8

Answers will vary.

UNIT 17 (pages 136–143)

1

2. (quite) → stressful
3. (extremely) → difficult
4. (Fortunately) → [entire sentence]
5. (really) → rural

6. (There) → live /(quietly) → live /(peacefully) →
live

7. (seldom) → turn on

8. (take) → daily /(soon) → get back

9. (occasionally) → see /(there) → welcome

10. (basically) → [entire sentence]

11. (really) → want

12. (very) → thoroughly /(thoroughly) → thought

13. (Rarely) → let

14. (Sadly) → [entire sentence]

15. (Now) → dreaming /(just) → dreaming

2

2. (never)—frequency

3. (sometimes)—frequency

4. (suddenly)—manner

5. (recently)—time

6. (soon)—time

7. (there)—place

8. (quickly)—manner

9. (differently)—manner

10. (carefully)—manner

11. (everywhere)—place

12. (occasionally)—frequency

13. (now)—time

14. (tomorrow)—time

3

2. Just	**15.** never
3. home	**16.** Never
4. almost	**17.** never
5. here	**18.** Obviously
6. downhill	**19.** just
7. completely	**20.** rarely
8. hardly	**21.** even
9. almost	**22.** just
10. scarcely	**23.** No way
11. ever	**24.** Little
12. downtown	**25.** one day
13. rarely	**26.** even
14. Not only	**27.** Only

4

2. But really he used up the state's money.

3. He put only his cronies in the best jobs.

4. He did everything he could for his cronies; he even paid for their so-called business trips.

5. He did merely the minimal work.

6. He simply appeared in his office, dispensed favors, and went out to play golf.

7. He just didn't care about the people of this state.

8. This state will be saved only if you elect Don Deare.

5

2. Seldom does he take a vacation.

3. Rarely is he able to spend much time with them, however.

4. Never does he neglect his family.

5. On no account would he accept a bribe.

6. Only then does he take action.

7. Little do people realize how many hours he has volunteered at the shelter for the homeless.

8. Never does he think of himself first.

9. Not only has he served the people very well as a civic volunteer, but he will do even more for them as a senator.

6

Situation 2: here he is

Situation 3: Here You Come Again

Situation 4: here I come

Situation 5: there lies the problem

Situation 6: There goes the president

7

Hello, soccer fans! We're coming ~~today to you~~ *to you today* from Starz Stadium, where we've been watching a fantastic soccer game— ~~rarely we~~ *rarely do we / we rarely* see soccer played like this! Both teams are in great shape, really ~~kicking up and down the field that ball~~ *kicking that ball up and down the field* —wow, this game is very exciting!

At halftime now, the score stands at 1–0. What a game! In the first half, Alfredo Brown scored a goal for the Panthers ~~as just~~ *just as* the game began. This is Brown's first season with the team—he's still a rookie—and the fans are really grateful to have him. A rookie ~~doesn't get usually~~ *usually doesn't get / doesn't usually get* many opportunities to be the star of the game, but Brown certainly has. He's scored at least one goal in every game that he's played, and he ~~scores often~~ *often scores* two or three. He has been playing ~~spectacular~~ *spectacularly*, there's no doubt about it! Even though it's ~~his only~~ *only his* first season, Brown has already made his mark in Panther history.

And for the Leopards—Lowell White, the goalie, stopped Brown from making three goals in the second quarter. ~~Brown even~~ *Even Brown* —the shining star of the Panthers—couldn't get the ball past White in this quarter. In that last goal that Brown attempted, White was hit in the chest by a ball

going 85 miles per hour. He was knocked down
and temporarily winded, but ~~he was not fortunately~~ *fortunately he was not*
injured. White got the Bailey Award last year for
being the most valuable player in the league, and
he surely deserved it.

And ~~they come here~~ *here they come* again, ladies and
gentlemen—the Panthers and the Leopards, the
top two teams of the league! There ~~Brown is~~, *is Brown*
waving to the crowd. Clearly, they love him.
That's his father over there on the right—see him
in the red hat, jumping up and down and
applauding ~~mad~~? *madly* And ~~here the Leopards come~~ *here come the Leopards*
—there's Lowell White, lookin' good!

We are just about to begin the second half in
this thriller of a game. ~~Seldom soccer is~~ *Soccer seldom is / Seldom is soccer* played as
beautifully as it is being played today, ladies and
gentlemen. Not only ~~this game is~~ *is this game* a thriller, but
each team is performing with true professional
skill. OK, there's the whistle, and the Leopards are
running down the field. . . .

8

Answers will vary.

UNIT 18 (pages 144–149)

1

A: Dr. Scope, just what *does* make a happy
family?

B: There is a cliché that all happy families
have some things in common.
contrast
While this may be trite, it is also true.

A: Really? What are these things?

B: Well, in happy families, *contrast* even though family
members may argue, they have a basic
concern for each other. Since every person
reason
needs to know that somebody really cares
for and about him or her, this is perhaps the
most important factor.

A: Is this caring enough to keep young people on
the road to productive lives, and certainly
away from non-social behavior?

B: No. Of course it's not so simple, but . . . a
person who feels connected to others is more
likely to act in socially acceptable ways,
contrast
whereas a person who does not feel connected
often acts in antisocial ways.

A: So, is being connected the principal factor?

B: It is very important.

A: Tell us what else is important.

B: *time* When family members support each other's
goals, the family feels united.

A: Give us an example.

B: Well, *condition* if a parent is hoping to be promoted at
work, everybody is supportive and shows
condition
interest. If a youngster is trying to make the
basketball team, the other family members
show encouragement and warmth.

A: What happens in times of trouble?

B: *time* When one family member is having trouble,
the others should exhibit concern and try to
help. Suppose, for example, that a family
member has been fired from a job. This
person may suddenly feel totally worthless in
contrast
society, although, of course, this is not true.
reason
In fact, precisely because this person doesn't
have a job, he or she needs to feel valued as a
human being.

A: So, is that the key word, *valued*?

B: I think it is. People need to feel valued,
appreciated. They also need to feel secure
among the family members. They need to
know that their families will always be there
condition
for them even if they are irritable, depressed,
ill, unemployed—or whatever.

A: Does the economic status of the family
matter?

B: Of course, economic stability is favorable. But
place
happy families exist wherever you look, in
all economic strata. And unhappy families as
well.

A: Well, thank you very much doctor. We
certainly feel a little more enlightened than we
did before.

2

2. as soon as the warmer weather arrives
3. Wherever a busy person travels
4. anywhere you shop
5. When you want
6. Even though he may already have
7. If your loved one loves
8. even if it's raining outside

2. As soon as
3. Until
4. Wherever
5. If
6. even though
7. Unless
8. while

2. When we turn to certain sports channels on TV, we see athletes jumping, diving, somersaulting over dangerous landscapes, and otherwise contorting themselves. *OR*
We see athletes jumping, diving, somersaulting over dangerous landscapes, and otherwise contorting themselves when we turn to certain sports channels on TV.

3. Because these athletes push themselves to extreme and dangerous levels, this category of sports is called "extreme sports." *OR*
This category of sports is called "extreme sports" because these athletes push themselves to extreme and dangerous levels.

4. Although extreme sports are dangerous, they are becoming more and more popular among young people all over the world. *OR*
Although they are becoming more and more popular among young people all over the world, extreme sports are dangerous.

5. As these sports are extreme and dangerous, many people think they should not be encouraged.

6. Even though extreme sports are not seen at the Olympic Games yet, there are twice-yearly competitive games showing extreme sports on some sports channels. *OR*
There are twice-yearly competitive games showing extreme sports on some sports channels, even though extreme sports are not seen at the Olympic Games yet.

7. Since "X" represents the word "extreme," these games are called "The X-Games." *OR*
These games are called "The X-Games," since "X" represents the word "extreme."

8. Since they first appeared on television in 1995, they have been increasingly popular. *OR*
They have been increasingly popular since they first appeared on television in 1995.

9. Wherever there are young people who want to compete in "real adventure," there will be more and more participants in extreme sports. *OR*
There will be more and more participants in extreme sports wherever there are young people who want to compete in "real adventure."

Do animals really have a sixth sense, one that warns them in advance of an imminent danger before ~~that~~ it occurs? Some people think so. When a tragic tsunami hit the coastlines of Asia on December 26, 2004, apparently many of the wild animals had already fled to safety on higher ground. For example, just before ~~X~~ the tsunami struck, a dozen elephants giving tourists rides *just north* ~~north just~~ of Phuket in Thailand began screaming and ran to a higher place. *Because / since* ~~Whereas~~ few elephants were found in the devastated areas after the tidal waves had receded, it is thought that most of them must have escaped in this manner.

Flamingos all flew away from their low-lying breeding areas on India's southern coast long before *the tsunami hit* ~~hit the tsunami~~, and zoo animals rushed back into their shelters wherever ~~that~~ they could, according to wildlife officials. What's more, rangers in Sri Lanka's Yala National Park report that hundreds of elephants, leopards, tigers, wild boar, deer, water buffalo, monkeys, and smaller mammals and reptiles survived *because* ~~unless~~ they had left the area. Likewise, although a few large turtles ~~they~~ have been found dead along the shore of Indonesia's Aceh province, the tsunami's impact on wildlife was "limited," say officials there. It appears that many animals survived because ~~X~~ they had left the area, while people survived *only if* ~~if only~~ they were able to find shelter or hold onto something large.

A scientist at the Bronx Zoo in New York says that animals can sense danger because they can detect subtle or abrupt shifts in the environment. "Earthquakes bring vibrational changes on land and in water, while storms cause electromagnetic changes in the atmosphere," he says. He adds that some animals have acute senses of hearing and smell—much sharper than humans'—and can pick up these changes wherever disasters are about to occur ~~there~~. Some fish, for instance, react to very weak earthquakes that even ~~X~~ people on land can't feel. Likewise, sharks go off to deeper waters as hurricanes approach, according to scientific reports about recent Florida hurricanes.

Even if / Although / Though / While
~~If even~~ there are many stories and some recorded data about animals' sharper senses, so far there is no generally accepted scientific truth about

a sixth sense in animals. Many people would, however, agree with this observation from a Danish survivor of the Asian tsunami: "Dogs are smarter than all of us. . . . they started running away up to the hilltops long before we even realized what was coming."

6

Answers will vary.

UNIT 19 (pages 150–156)

1

While in the car
When in a boat
Riding in a boat
On seeing another boat
Having docked
Being able to swim
While in the water
Having learned these rules
When riding bicycles
Suffering from severe sunburn
Before going out in the sun
Not wanting to wear a hat
When buying sunglasses for children

2

2. After having rained
3. While driving
4. hitting
5. crashing
6. Stunned
7. Being dazed
8. Being
9. Before realizing
10. having crashed
11. After acknowledging
12. waiting
13. Having arrived
14. Not having been
15. Since notifying

3

2. Having been told . . . / Told that vitamin C, vitamin E, and beta-carotene greatly reduce cancer risk, people began buying these nutrients in large quantities.
3. Having been informed . . . / Informed that taking one aspirin a day lowers the chances of having a heart attack, people began taking aspirin.
4. Having learned that one bowl of whole-grain cereal per day may have a beneficial effect on the heart and circulatory system, many people now eat more whole-grain cereal.
5. Hoping to lower their cholesterol levels, people minimize their intake of animal fats.
6. Knowing that fiber in the diet is excellent for digestion, people are consuming more fresh fruit, vegetables, and whole wheat products.

7. Believing that eating a lot of fish will raise their intelligence level, some people eat a lot of fish.
8. Having known for a long time that too much salt and sugar is unhealthful, people buy a lot of salt-free and sugar-free products.
9. Realizing that they can contribute to their own good health, people eat much more knowledgeably than they used to.

4

2. c 3. b 4. c 5. a 6. b 7. b 8. c
9. a 10. c 11. a 12. b

5

Celia Cruz was one of Latin music's most respected and beloved vocalists. ~~Sing~~ *Singing* only in her native Spanish language, Cruz was world-renowned. In addition to her great popularity—for example, a street in Miami is named after her—she was critically acclaimed, ~~having receiving~~ *receiving / having received* dozens of honors. Displayed in a permanent collection of the Smithsonian Museum, Cruz's distinctive outfits—her red, white, and orange polka-dot dress, her nine-inch heels, and her extravagant wigs—get smiles from visitors every day, just as she did throughout her life.

~~Having born~~ *Born* in a small village in Cuba, Cruz loved music from early childhood. Many evenings, while singing lullabies to her younger sisters and brothers, Celia's voice would attract neighbors who wanted to come in to listen. She sang in school productions and community gatherings as well, impressing all those who heard her voice. ~~Having being encouraged~~ *Having been encouraged / Encouraged* by a cousin to enter local talent shows, Cruz did so and began winning right away. At the same time, when ~~taking~~ *(she was) taken* to cabarets and nightclubs by an aunt, she discovered the world of professional music. Although her family wanted her to be a teacher, she continued to be lured by music.

In the 1940s, after giving up the idea of becoming a schoolteacher, she began to sing on the radio and enrolled in Cuba's Conservatory of Music. There she found inspiration in Afro-Cuban dance music, embracing the mambo, cha-cha, and modern salsa, among other types of music, and later, modern salsa. ~~After joined~~ *After joining / After having joined / After she joined / After she had joined* a dance band called la Sonora Matancera, she toured throughout the world with them, and in 1962 she married the band's trumpet player, Pedro Knight. Not ~~wanted~~ *wanting* to remain in Cuba because of political reasons, Cruz and Knight, along with the band, moved to Mexico. Soon afterwards, they moved to the United States, where she embarked on her solo career, although she teamed up with other artists from time to time.

Loved for her high energy, her voice, her talent and charisma, Cruz transmitted the joy of music to her millions of fans. ~~Remember~~ *Remembering* her father's wishes, in a 1997 interview she said that, although not having ~~fulfilling~~ *fulfilled* her father's wish for her to be a teacher, she fulfilled that wish through her music. While ~~she singing~~ *she sang / was singing*, she taught people about her culture and the happiness found in just living life. While ~~performed~~ *she performed / performing*, she wanted people to feel their hearts sing and their spirits soar.

6

Answers will vary.

UNIT 20 (pages 157–164)

1

Good evening, ladies and gentlemen. We are here to bring you the latest news from Hollywood. <u>First</u>, a major new studio has been created. The three biggest motion picture producers have just joined forces to form a new studio. <u>As a result</u>, Big Three Productions, as it is going to be named, will be the largest studio ever in Hollywood. <u>Moreover</u>, it has more money behind it than any studio in Hollywood has ever had. <u>In addition</u>, seven megastars have joined the group as limited partners; <u>therefore</u>, they will have a financial interest in the success of the company. Big Three Productions is expected to produce excellent financial results even at the beginning. There are, <u>however</u>, several lawsuits pending against the three partners, due to the complicated business dealings they had with their previous studios. <u>For instance</u>, the ex-wife of one of the partners has brought a lawsuit against him; she claims that he and their previous studio owe her $7 million for her starring role in *Turner Towers*. She left the movie set because she couldn't get along with the director; <u>nevertheless</u>, she says that she was prevented from making a living.

<u>Next</u>, we have reports that movie queen Rosalinda Rock has finally found happiness. She and actor Fox Craft were married secretly last month in a small town in Nevada. There had been reports that Fox was involved with an Italian starlet, <u>but</u> these reports have turned out to be false. Rosalinda and Fox are on their honeymoon now; <u>afterwards</u>, they'll be in residence at their home in Sun Valley, <u>or</u> at their beach house in Santa Monica. Fox gave Rosalinda a diamond-and-emerald necklace as a wedding present; he had already given her a ten-carat diamond ring several weeks earlier. Rosalinda says she wants to have many children and stay home, at one of her homes, to enjoy domestic life. She's going off to Tahiti right after the honeymoon, <u>nonetheless</u>, for several months on location.

<u>Finally</u>, nobody can predict this year who the winners of the Academy Awards are going to be. <u>First</u>, the pictures this year seem better than ever before. <u>For example</u>, the adventure story *Running in Space* has stunned everyone with its special effects, <u>and</u> it has impressed the critics with its incredible plot. It's a definite contender for the best picture award. <u>Likewise</u>, *I Remember When*—a beautiful piece of nostalgia—moved even the most macho of men to tears. <u>On the other hand</u>, the award could go to any one of several fine comedies, <u>or</u> the brilliant horror movie *Drackenstein* might be the first of its genre to win.

The suspense over the Academy Awards is tremendous, <u>and</u> everybody is eagerly awaiting the big night. <u>Meanwhile</u>, join us again every night at 9:00 to learn more of what's really going on Around the Stars.

2

2. but	8. otherwise
3. As a result	9. so
4. because	10. Moreover
5. Although	11. in addition to
6. For example	12. Meanwhile
7. also	

3

2. i **3.** a **4.** g **5.** b **6.** h **7.** c **8.** d **9.** e

4

Now I'm really worried about you. I'm the one who's always asking for advice,

(~~and~~ / but / yet) this time, I'm the one who's
1.
giving it. I'm the one who is always in a mess;
(however / ~~besides~~ / instead), this time you're the
2.
one in trouble.

(First / ~~Next~~ / ~~Finally~~), no matter what,
3.
you have to get a hold of yourself.
(~~Yet~~ / ~~Therefore~~ / Otherwise), you are going to
4.
spiral downward and feel worse and worse.
(Furthermore / ~~In contrast~~ / In addition), you
5.
won't be able to do anything well—studying,
(for instance / for example / ~~nevertheless~~), or even
6.
winning at cards—in this depressed mood that
you're in. (And / ~~But~~ / Plus) Lisa or any other
7.
young woman you may meet is going to find you
very boring, (~~moreover~~ / ~~however~~ / so) you'll
8.
definitely find yourself without a girlfriend.
(Therefore / ~~Otherwise~~ / ~~Nor~~), even though you
9.
feel terrible, you've got to get out in the world
again. (~~However~~ / For instance / ~~Nevertheless~~),
10.
you mentioned that other girls had asked you to
dinner—you should accept their invitations. Who
knows? You might have a wonderful dinner.
(Plus / Besides / ~~Instead~~), you might even find a
11.
really pleasant relationship.

Now, enough about you. Let's get back
to me. I got fired. I was doing everything right,
(~~finally~~ / but / ~~so~~) I still got fired. It was a terrible
12.
experience. (~~Thus~~ / Besides / ~~Nor~~), it couldn't
13.
have happened at a worse time: I'd just found out
my landlord is raising the rent.
I'll hang in there, (and / ~~though~~ / ~~therefore~~)
14.
I'll let you know when I find a new job.
(In the meantime / ~~Therefore~~ / ~~So~~), I hope to have
15.
some better news from you soon.

5

2. b **3.** b **4.** c **5.** c **6.** a **7.** c **8.** c

6

Additional answers may be possible.

I'm the center on my basketball team. I like to
play basketball for a lot of reasons:
First
~~Next~~, I like the teamwork. It really feels good
to be part of a group whose members depend

For example / For instance
on each other. ~~In contrast~~, when I throw the ball
to one of my teammates, I know that he will
almost certainly catch it. We have practiced
and
hundreds of times ~~but~~ have perfected our skills
pretty well. Thus, our score is due not only to his
tossing the ball into the basketball hoop, but in
part to my throwing, and in part to each member
of the team.

Second, I like the competition. I like the
and
feeling of playing to win, ~~or~~ I like the feeling of
fighting the other team, too. It makes the
adrenaline rush when you know that you have to
consequently / therefore / as a result
fight hard; ~~otherwise~~, your heart beats faster, you
breathe more rapidly, and you sweat a lot.

Third, I like the physical exercise. I think
pushing myself to my physical limit is good for my
body. I am not afraid of overdoing the exercise,
nor do I have fears of being hurt during a game;
however / still
~~therefore~~, I know that basketball players
sometimes get hurt, so I—as well as my
teammates—try to move in ways that avoid injury.

Finally, I like the glory. I love it when the
crowd roars to encourage us, and I love it when
I hear the cheerleaders shouting my name.
In addition / Besides / Plus / Likewise
~~However~~, it sure makes a guy feel important to be
recognized around town as a big hero.

Are there any drawbacks? Yes. It's terrific to
although / but / though
play basketball, ~~because~~ there are some negative
however / nevertheless / still / on the other hand
aspects. Being part of a team is great; ~~furthermore~~,
you have to practice too much and you don't have
much of a private life. Playing in competition is
but
exciting; ~~moreover~~ you don't get much chance to
relax. Getting all that physical exercise feels
however / nevertheless / still / on the other hand
wonderful; ~~therefore~~, you might get seriously hurt.
In fact, there's a negative aspect to each of the
but
things I like about basketball, ~~and~~ these
drawbacks are relatively unimportant.

In conclusion, I totally enjoy being a
because
basketball player ~~although~~ I love the teamwork,
the competition, the physical exercise, and the
glory.

7

Answers will vary.

UNIT 21 (pages 165–171)

1

A: Is it really true <u>that a plant will grow better if you talk to it</u>?

B: Yes. Studies have shown <u>how much better plants grow when they are talked to</u>.

A: But, plants don't have sound receptors or nervous systems, so can you tell us <u>why that is</u>?

B: Scientists know <u>that plants aren't responding to the specific words people say</u>. <u>What happens</u> is very interesting: When you talk, you breathe out carbon dioxide and water vapor. <u>That plants need carbon dioxide and water in order</u> to grow is basic. They get more of these two vital nutrients from your breath. And, sound waves from your voice cause plant cells to vibrate. Experiments have demonstrated <u>that certain types and strengths of sound can affect plants</u>. These sounds can cause plants to grow better—or worse—than usual. An interesting result, for example, is <u>what plants have done after being exposed to classical music</u>: They grew thick, healthy leaves and developed good roots.

A: Only classical music? It makes a difference <u>if the plants hear classical music or other kinds of music</u>?

B: Well, it's interesting <u>that it does seem to matter</u>. Plants seem to care about <u>what kind of music they "hear."</u> Jazz has also had a beneficial effect. And plants exposed to country music had normal growth. But, plants that were exposed to rock music did very poorly. Their root development was so terrible that the plants began to die.

A: No way! Do plants actually know <u>who they are listening to</u>—<u>whether they are listening to Mozart or to Green Day</u>?

B: Not exactly "know." <u>What they do</u> is sense the vibrations, and apparently they can differentiate the types of rhythm and number of decibels.

A: Hmmm. Well, here's <u>what I think</u>: <u>The fact that you talk to your plants</u> is good because it means <u>that you are paying attention to them</u>. <u>What you are doing</u> is giving them the water and food and pruning they need, and not letting them die of neglect.

B: That's true. The issue of <u>whether plants live or die</u> depends on their receiving nutrients. But the answer to your original question— <u>whether or not plants actually *do better*</u> when you talk to them—is definitely yes.

2

2. I have to forget about Lisa
3. this is not going to be easy
4. I can't forget about her
5. I am not receptive to meeting people
6. I get my life in order
7. I should think about other things
8. you must be responsible on the job
9. you have always been too casual about your work
10. you adopt a better attitude
11. you won't invest in any more iffy deals
12. we are truthful with each other

3

2. the Olympics/they will be held
3. the symbol for ozone/it is
4. *numeracy*/it means
5. the biggest bone in the body/it is
6. some fish/they swim

4

2. whether (or not) / if the stores will be closed
3. whether (or not) / if the buses are running
4. whether (or not) / if there is enough food
5. Whether (or not) / if the roads are safe
6. whether (or not) / if the electricity is going to go off
7. whether (or not) / if anyone wants to play Scrabble
8. whether (or not) / if he has to go to work
9. whether (or not) / if Aunt Catherine's plane will be flying
10. whether (or not) / if the schools are going to be closed tomorrow, too.

5

2. what he said to Marla/her
3. That Marla/she is upset
4. where Marla/she is now
5. What Marla/she is going to do
6. whether (or not) Marla/she is going to get fired / whether Marla/she is going to get fired (or not) / if Marla/she is going to get fired (or not)
7. whether (or not) Marla/she is going to be arrested / whether Marla/she is going to be arrested (or not) / if Marla/she is going to be arrested (or not)
8. what you are
9. What we are talking about

6

Is Mavis Gordon, the Chief Financial Officer of Exia, Inc., really guilty of allowing employees to produce false financial records? That's what ~~is the jury~~ *the jury is* going to have to determine at this trial. They're going to have to decide what ~~did~~ she knew and when she ~~did know~~ *knew* it. Today the District Attorney asked Gordon several questions about her specific role in keeping Exia's books. First he wanted to know how long ~~had she~~ *she had* been working at the company, and when she became Chief Financial Officer. Then he asked her ~~that~~ if all financial information was routed by her personally. When she said, "No," he asked her which parts she had indeed seen.

This is where ~~does the picture become~~ *the picture becomes* unclear. Gordon says that she trusted her assistants and that she never knew that they were keeping false bookkeeping records. Those false records were only for the public to see; they did not reflect what ~~X~~ was really happening: that some officers were in fact embezzling money from the company—that is, stealing the money and hiding it.

The prosecution believes that Gordon knew the records were false and collaborated with the perpetrators of the crime. The defense, on the other hand, claims that Gordon always acted in good faith and had no reason to distrust her assistants.

When ~~did Gordon find~~ *Gordon found* out about the false records is important. If she learned about the deception only after the case became public, then she is certainly not guilty of any criminal action. If, however, she knew about what ~~were her assistants~~ *her assistants were* doing before the case became public, then she is indeed guilty of fraud.

~~If~~ *Whether* or not Gordon herself embezzled money is not the point at issue. The point is whether or not ~~was she~~ *she was* actually aware of what ~~X~~ was happening in her company. That ~~will the truth~~ *the truth will* be revealed in testimony over the next several days is certain. The judge has reminded the jurors of the fact that a person is innocent until proven guilty. If the prosecution is going to convict Mavis Gordon, they will have to show indisputable evidence ~~what~~ *that* she knew—before it became public—about the bookkeeping fraud being committed on her watch.

7

Answers will vary.

UNIT 22 (pages 172–179)

1

The monthly meting of the Board of Directors of the Towers Condominium was held on the first Thursday of the month, as customary.

The meeting was begun at 6:40 P.M. by Ms. Janet Jones, President, who said, "The meeting is called to order. Welcome Board members, unit owners, Mr. Bitter, and guests."

Reports of Officers and Committees
1. *East Side Homeowners Association.* Mrs. Pantini <u>informed the Board that the County Commission had rejected the proposal for a new office high-rise building on our street.</u> She also <u>remarked that a new Foodsworth Supermarket is being considered for this area.</u>
2. *The Towers Parking Committee.* Dr. Gardner <u>reported that a new system is going into effect starting on the first of next month,</u> and he <u>said all the residents would be receiving new I.D. decals.</u> He <u>told everyone to place the new decals in the front windows of their cars.</u>

Old Business
1. "Bids for repairs to the elevators are being submitted," reported Board member Mr. Green. He <u>stated that formal proposals would be considered before the next meeting.</u>
2. "The office secretary's job still hasn't been filled," the manager reported. He <u>asked if anybody knew of a good secretary.</u> Then he <u>asked where a good one could be found,</u> and <u>reminded the Board that the job has been vacant for six weeks.</u> Ms. Sloane <u>wondered whether the salary was too low</u> and Mr. Bitter <u>replied that he had placed a new ad on the Internet, this time with a higher salary.</u>
3. The manager <u>informed the Board that the water intrusion repairs are still not finished.</u> Mr. Evans <u>asked who was directly responsible for the long delay</u> and <u>told the Board that the Association should file a lawsuit against the contractor.</u>

New Business
John C. Algernon from InterRes, a satellite company, and his associate Alan Evans, presented a short proposal for a new system for our

building. Mr. Algernon said that all our cable, telephone, and Internet needs could be met by installing his system, and said it would be much more economical than the systems we have. He asked the group who would be interested in the new system and asked where they could be contacted during the day.

Closing
Ms. Jones asked whether there was any further business, and the answer was negative. The meeting was adjourned at 8:05 P.M.

disabled. The remaining 41 percent said that they weren't sure.

Question 4. Are taxes too high?
When asked ~~if taxes were too high,~~ only 16 percent claimed that they were. Astonishingly, 38 percent stated that taxes were not high enough and that people would have to pay more for necessary services in the future. The rest (46%) didn't ~~told~~ ^say^ what they thought.

Question 5. Is the quality of life better or worse now than it was 10 years ago?
When asked how the quality of their lives was now, compared with what it had been 10 years ago, the population was again divided about half and half. 48 percent ~~said *Polls Today*~~ ^said / told *Polls Today*^ that the quality of their lives had improved over the last decade, and 46 percent said that it had deteriorated. A remaining 6 percent reported that they didn't have an opinion.

7

Answers will vary.

UNIT 23 (pages 180–188)

1

The dictionary defines *chocoholic* as a person who has a near obsession for chocolate. The world is full of chocoholics. <u>Yet, if an unusual sequence of events had not occurred, these people would probably never have tasted chocolate.</u>

Chocolate was unknown outside of the Americas until the 16th century. When the Spanish arrived in Mexico in the early 1500s, they discovered that the Aztec Indians there drank a delicious, dark, foamy beverage called *chocolatl*, brewed from the beans of the native cacao plant. These cacao beans were so highly valued in the area that they were used by the natives as money in the marketplaces; a pumpkin could be bought for 4 cacao beans, for example, and a rabbit could be bought for 10. The Aztecs evidently had chocoholics as well as chocolate. Their king, Montezuma, normally drank 50 pitchers of *chocolatl* a day; it is said that when he didn't, he felt a very strong physical need for it.

The explorer Hernán Cortés wrote in a letter to the Spanish emperor Charles V that he had discovered "a divine drink . . . which builds up resistance and fights fatigue." It's a good thing for the chocolate lovers of the world that Hernán Cortés liked chocolate. <u>If he hadn't, the delicious substance might never have crossed the ocean back</u> <u>to Spain with him.</u> Chocolate soon became popular in Spain as a thick, sugared, chilled beverage and later appeared elsewhere in Europe. In mid-17th-century London, chocolate houses, like coffee houses, sprang up; however, only the aristocrats could enjoy the drink because of its high cost. <u>If chocolate hadn't been so expensive, the common people could have enjoyed it much sooner.</u>

Doctors of the era reported that chocolate was an effective medicine which imparted energy, among other things. When people wanted to feel stronger quickly, they could take some chocolate. Chocolate contains theobromine, a substance similar to caffeine; it is actually the theobromine which causes people to feel energized after drinking chocolate. <u>If chocolate didn't contain theobromine, it wouldn't have the stimulating effect that it has.</u>

Chocolate was primarily a beverage until the 1800s, when a Swiss chocolatier discovered that chocolate combined well with milk solids. <u>If this chocolatier hadn't made that discovery, chocolate would not have evolved into its solid form. And if chocolate had not evolved into its solid form, we would not have the chocolate candy, and chocolate cakes, and chocolate cookies that we enjoy so much today.</u>

Today, 75 percent of the world's cacao comes from Africa, and the rest comes from Central America, Ecuador, and Brazil. But, chocolate is heavily consumed in countries all over the world, in countries far from the sources of cacao. <u>Clearly, if world trade were not so well developed, chocolate lovers worldwide would not be able to indulge themselves as easily as they can.</u>

For all the pleasure that chocolate imparts, it does have some bad effects. It contains a lot of fats and sugar, so when people eat too much of it, they can develop or worsen conditions such as hardening of the arteries or diabetes. <u>Doctors have been telling patients for a long time that if their fat and sugar intake were lower, they would be healthier.</u> However, these warnings do not prevent chocoholics from consuming what they love. Says one chocoholic who partakes daily: <u>"Quite frankly, if I had a day without chocolate, it would be like a day without sunshine."</u>

2

2. (Chocolate) was brought back to Europe by the Spanish explorers. (It) is popular today.
3. (Air conditioning) was developed in the 20th century. (Places like Florida) are popular locations to live.

4. (The earth) is not flat / (The earth) is round.
   (Columbus) discovered the New World.
5. (Dinosaurs) don't roam the earth (anymore).
   (Humans) are living today.
6. (Frogs) don't have wings. (They) can't fly.

3

2. d 3. b 4. i 5. n 6. g 7. m 8. c
9. f 10. j 11. a 12. e 13. h 14. l

4

2. If Saudi Arabia were not an oil-rich country
3. Canada would not import oranges
4. If Thailand didn't have a tropical climate /
   If Thailand had a colder climate
5. Brazil wouldn't have become a large producer
   of coffee
6. it wouldn't have 11 time zones
7. If the Chinese government hadn't made huge
   efforts to save the panda

5

A 2. I met the right man, I would have a differ-
      ent feeling about it
   3. I didn't have a lot of friends, I would be
      lonely
   4. I didn't like my job, I would be unhappy
   5. (that) people would leave me alone
   6. I could meet the perfect man tomorrow
   7. (that) I had it all / I could have it all
B 8. they start
   9. I often don't say it
  10. nobody will understand you
  11. I don't speak
  12. a man and a woman are in a conversation
  13. who usually talks first
  14. who usually speaks more

6

2. wouldn't have had to eat
3. wouldn't have been
4. never would/would never have suffered
5. had met
6. had never met
7. hadn't/wouldn't have happened
8. hadn't made
9. would have passed

7

What is the situation?
Robert and Cynthia are good friends and are both
lawyers at the Marks and Hobbs law firm. They
both hope to be selected as partners at the end of

the year. If a person ~~will be~~ *is* selected to be a
partner, he or she will become a part-owner of the
law firm, and therefore, ~~would had~~ *will have* a secure future
there. Robert and Cynthia's supervisor, Henry
Marks, has told Robert that he is likely to get a
partnership at the end of the year, but that
Cynthia isn't. *Should Robert tell Cynthia this?*

What should Robert do?
- *He should tell.* If Cynthia ~~had~~ *does* not become a
  partner, she will have no future in the firm.
  Robert and Cynthia are good friends, and they
  should be honest with each other. If Cynthia
  ~~will find~~ *finds* out the truth now, she can get another
  job. Furthermore, if Robert ~~would~~ *does* not tell her,
  he will have to lie to Cynthia for the rest of the
  year. In addition, Robert should think, "If the
  situation ~~is~~ *were* reversed, would I want to know the
  truth?" The answer is, "Yes."
- *He shouldn't tell.* If he ~~has~~ told her, it would
  destroy the confidence that his boss has in him.
  In fact, if Robert ~~would~~ broke the confidence, he
  himself might not be promoted; Henry would
  ~~lost~~ *lose* confidence in him.

What happened?
Robert told Cynthia, who confronted Henry.
Henry, of course, was angry at Robert for
breaking a trust, and he told Robert that he was
no longer a candidate for the promotion.

What does everyone think now?
- *Robert:* What a mistake! I wish I ~~don't tell~~ *hadn't told*
  Cynthia! She could have worked for the
  remainder of the year if I ~~haven't~~ *hadn't* told her. Then,
  at the end of the year she could leave the firm if
  she wanted to. If I hadn't told her, I ~~will~~ *would* be in
  line for a promotion now. Now neither of us will
  be promoted.
- *Cynthia:* I really appreciate Robert's friendship,
  but I'm really sorry he has lost his own
  opportunity. If I ~~am~~ *were* Robert and the situation
  ~~be~~ *were / had been* reversed—would I have told him? Maybe not.
- *Henry:* I never should have told Robert
  anything. If I had kept the information to
  myself, none of this would ~~had~~ *have* happened. Now
  I have lost the trust and confidence of two good

colleagues. I wish I ~~have~~ ^had^ their confidence again, but that's not possible. If only it ~~is~~ ^were^ easy to be the boss of this law firm!

Answers will vary.

UNIT 24 (pages 189–196)

1

Without the simple little tool   IMP
that we have   (circled)
Were there no can openers   INV
Were there no can openers   INV
But for canned tuna   IMP
A better way to open cans had to be found;
    if not   IMP
it had to be used correctly. If not   IMP
Had the U.S. military not discovered this primitive
    can opener   INV
there be   (circled)
Without canned goods   IMP
can openers were invented; otherwise   INP
should there be an emergency   INV
that every family have   (circled)

2

2. not fought; would not have been known
3. might not have won
4. would not have grown
5. not succeeded; would have succeeded
6. would not have developed
7. lived; might have been
8. would have already become

3

2. we would have to use our fingers to eat
3. not been discovered, we wouldn't have electric lights, movies, television, or computers
4. existed 100 years ago, people would have traveled extensively then
5. not available throughout the world, fashion, music, and basic values would not be very similar in many places
6. not been developed, businesses wouldn't be able to obtain the data they need to function in today's world
7. the general public wouldn't have easy access to extensive information
8. have a cellular phone, he or she would not be able to communicate from remote places

4

2. Julius Caesar not conquered several areas of the world, people in those areas would not speak "Romance" languages.
3. the Spanish and Portuguese settled North America, people there would not speak English, but Spanish or Portuguese OR the English not settled North America, people there wouldn't speak English
4. blue jeans not been invented in 1849, everyone all over the world wouldn't be wearing blue jeans today
5. penicillin not been discovered in 1928, hundreds of millions of lives would have been lost OR penicillin not been discovered in 1928, hundreds of millions of lives would not have been saved.
6. Dolly the sheep not been cloned in 1997, certain amazing scientific possibilities and troubling ethical questions would not have been raised
7. there gravity in a space ship, objects wouldn't float in the air there
8. the polar ice caps melt, certain coastal areas might be flooded

5

2. that drivers stay on the left side of the road
3. that people remove their shoes before going inside a house
4. that people keep their shoes on
5. that people not eat pork products
6. that a sick person be treated with modern medicine
7. that a sick person use herbal remedies
8. that a waiter be summoned by whistling
9. that a waiter not be summoned by whistling
10. that a traveler learn about customs in various places

6

I have often fantasized about the perfect world. It would be perfect not only for my family and me, but for everyone.

First of all, ~~we were~~ ^were we^ living in a perfect world, there would be food for everyone. No one would be starving or without regular sources of food. Second, in this perfect world, everything would ~~been~~ ^be^ clean and free of pollution. With clean air and toxin-free water, humans, animals, and plants

stay / have stayed
would ~~stayed~~ healthy. Third, all diseases would be
would
conquered; we ~~will~~ be free of cancer, AIDS, and
heart disease. Without those diseases, people could
live
~~lived~~ longer and be free from terrible suffering.
If scientists had / Had scientists
~~Scientists had~~ already discovered a cure for these
diseases, we could now be anticipating a much
longer life span. Fourth, were the world in perfect
would
condition, there ~~will~~ be no crime. Societal and
psychological factors would not breed the violence
that they do. And last, there would be no wars.
All countries and all peoples would live together,
harmoniously, as one.

While these goals may appear unrealistic,
it would be wise not to abandon them. Had
diplomats abandoned the idea of one world,
wouldn't
we ~~don't~~ have the United Nations today. Had
would
scientists given up their search for cures, we ~~will~~
not have found the means to conquer polio,
tuberculosis, some types of pneumonia, and many
bacteria-caused diseases. Had civic-minded
would
individuals been less tenacious, we ~~did~~ not have
cleaned up the cities and water and air as much
we not
as we have. Had ~~not we~~ learned and taught better

methods of agriculture and food distribution,
many more people would be starving today.
were
What if there ~~are~~ a universal law like this:
All the *haves*—those people who *have* a decent life
and more than enough material things—must
make concrete contributions to a perfect world?
Local governments would require that citizens
give
~~gave~~ a specified amount of time or money each
year to a recognized community project. What if
it were required by law that young people
study
~~studying~~ the histories of all major cultures?
Knowing about other cultures would ~~have~~ expand
people's minds and help them to understand each
other better. Would such compulsory programs
work? They might. They would, hopefully, help
the citizens of the world to think of others who
live in different situations. It is absolutely essential
be
that hope ~~is~~ expressed not only in words, but also
will
in actions; otherwise, the world ~~would~~ not be a
better place tomorrow than it is today.

7

Answers will vary.

Test: Units 1–3

PART ONE

Circle the letter of the correct answer to complete each sentence.

Example

Dolphins, _____ porpoises, are well known for their ability to delight humans with their antics. **A B Ⓒ D**

(**A**) alike   (**C**) like
(**B**) that they are like   (**D**) which are alike

1. Construction of the Brooklyn Bridge, the first steel-wire suspension bridge in the world, _____ in 1869 but wasn't finished until 1893. **A B C D**

 (**A**) was beginning   (**C**) began
 (**B**) has begun   (**D**) beginning

2. By the time the monorail is completed next year, the taxpayers _____ over $22 million for a transportation system that is already obsolete. **A B C D**

 (**A**) will spend   (**C**) will have spent
 (**B**) will be spending   (**D**) will have been spending

3. Since the use of antibiotics _____ widespread, certain types of pneumonia and streptococcal infections are no longer as terrifying as they once were. **A B C D**

 (**A**) was becoming   (**C**) had become
 (**B**) has become   (**D**) becomes

4. By the time the ancient Egyptian civilization began to flourish more than 5,000 years ago, the onion _____ a staple food throughout the Middle East for many years. **A B C D**

 (**A**) had already been   (**C**) has already been
 (**B**) was already   (**D**) would have been

5. Because the river _____ steadily since Sunday, the residents of the area have been advised to prepare for flood conditions. **A B C D**

 (**A**) rose   (**C**) is rising
 (**B**) had risen   (**D**) has been rising

6. The art museum is not being kept up properly. It is falling down in some places, and it _____ a new roof. **A B C D**

 (**A**) needs   (**C**) needed
 (**B**) is needing   (**D**) was needing

7. Astonishingly, in 1998 the citizens of Minnesota elected a governor who _____ a professional wrestler.   **A B C D**

   (**A**) would be   (**C**) have been
   (**B**) used to be   (**D**) both A and B

8. Although the use of popular computers exploded throughout the world in the 1990s, academics _____ by computer since the early 1970s.   **A B C D**

   (**A**) communicated   (**C**) are communicating
   (**B**) had been   (**D**) used to communicate
        communicating

9. Small children who witnessed Halley's Comet in 1986 might see it again when it _____ in the skies in 2061.   **A B C D**

   (**A**) is appearing   (**C**) will be appearing
   (**B**) will appear   (**D**) appears

10. By analyzing historical and current data, meteorologists can predict the number of hurricanes that _____ in the Caribbean in any given year.   **A B C D**

    (**A**) will appear   (**C**) are appearing
    (**B**) are going to appear (**D**) both A and B

PART TWO

Each sentence has four underlined words or phrases. The four underlined parts of the sentence are marked A, B, C, and D. Circle the letter of the <u>one</u> underlined word or phrase that is NOT CORRECT.

Example

People in <u>every part</u> of the world now <u>readily</u> and easily <u>communicates</u>   **A B Ⓒ D**
         A   B   C
<u>by means</u> of electronic mail.
  D

11. Because the beaches <u>are eroding</u> at an alarming rate for the <u>past</u> 10 years,   **A B C D**
                             A   B

    the state government <u>no longer</u> <u>permits</u> building within 100 yards of the
                             C   D

    coastal area.

12. The Rosetta Stone, which <u>is</u> a large piece of stone that priests <u>have inscribed</u>   **A B C D**
                            A   B

    more than 2,000 years ago, <u>was</u> discovered by Napoleon's troops in 1799
                                      C

    and <u>has provided</u> scholars with the key to deciphering Egyptian hieroglyphics.
         D

13. The Mayan Indians, archaeologists <u>are believing</u>, <u>originated</u> around 1000 B.C.   **A B C D**
                                     A   B

    in northern Guatemala, where evidence of an early agricultural people

    <u>has been</u> <u>found</u>.
      C   D

14. Before the construction of the English Chunnel, which <u>connects</u> France and   **A B C D**
                A

  England, most people <u>didn't</u> <u>think</u> that travel by land between the two
           B   C

  countries <u>will</u> be possible before the 21st century.
       D

15. Look! The baby <u>is tasting</u> his new cereal, and he <u>thinks</u> that it <u>is tasting</u> <u>good</u>!   **A B C D**
         A   B   C D

16. When the earthquake <u>occurred</u> at 3:49 A.M., most people in the city <u>slept</u> in   **A B C D**
           A   B

  their beds at home and so <u>escaped</u> the injuries that a few <u>suffered</u> from
            C   D

  collapsing bridges and crumbling highways.

17. It now <u>seems</u> <u>clearly</u> that the bus driver <u>was not</u> at fault when his bus <u>collided</u>   **A B C D**
     A B   C   D

  with a car on the highway.

18. During the past 15 years, retail sales from companies with an Internet   **A B C D**

  presence <u>were quadrupling</u>; it <u>appears</u> that people <u>are taking</u> advantage of
       A   B   C

  the great convenience of <u>shopping</u> from home.
            D

19. <u>By</u> the time the sailors in the famous Whitbread competition <u>reach</u> their final   **A B C D**
  A   B

  destination, they <u>will be traveling</u> over ocean waters <u>for</u> more than six
          C   D

  months.

20. When Dahlia <u>speaks</u>, you <u>hear</u> a very light accent; it <u>is sounding</u> like she   **A B C D**
       A   B   C

  <u>comes</u> from a country somewhere in the Middle East.
   D

Test: Units 4–6

PART ONE

Circle the letter of the correct answer to complete each sentence.

Example

Dolphins, _____ porpoises, are well known for their ability to delight humans with their antics.

A B Ⓒ D

(**A**) alike   (**C**) like
(**B**) that they are like   (**D**) which are alike

1. Although many spectators believed that the Australian gymnast, with her amazing flexibility and control, _____ the gold medal, the Olympic judges awarded it to the Romanian instead.

   A B C D

   (**A**) must have won   (**C**) had to win
   (**B**) should have won   (**D**) won

2. Before the construction of the Panama Canal, ships _____ around the tip of South America to get to the Pacific Ocean from the Atlantic Ocean.

   A B C D

   (**A**) should have traveled   (**C**) had to travel
   (**B**) must travel   (**D**) have traveled

3. It seems obvious, when looking at a map, that the eastern part of Brazil _____ connected to Africa long ago when the earth was forming.

   A B C D

   (**A**) must be   (**C**) should have been
   (**B**) must have been   (**D**) might be

4. The mayor told the townspeople that _____ the water until the laboratory declared it safe again.

   A B C D

   (**A**) they didn't have to drink   (**C**) they'd better not drink
   (**B**) they'd rather not drink   (**D**) they must not have drunk

5. It is generally agreed that when you travel in countries other than your own, you _____ conform to the local customs as much as possible.

   A B C D

   (**A**) could   (**C**) may
   (**B**) might   (**D**) should

6. The financial advisor told her client that he _____ invest in a money market fund or he _____ invest in municipal bonds—either way would be safe.

   A B C D

   (**A**) could / could   (**C**) could / must
   (**B**) must / must   (**D**) must / could

7. Residents of the apartment complex _____ rent a reserved parking space at $75 per month if they wish.

    A B C D

(**A**) must   (**C**) might
(**B**) may   (**D**) have got to

8. Sarah hasn't always lived in San Francisco, _____?

    A B C D

(**A**) does she   (**C**) hasn't she
(**B**) did she   (**D**) has she

9. No one believed Henry's story about having a twin brother, but it turns out that he actually _____ a twin brother, who committed the crime and is now in jail.

    A B C D

(**A**) does have   (**C**) has had
(**B**) did have   (**D**) does

10. A: I wonder if the officers of the company will like my idea.
    B: _____! It's a great idea!

    A B C D

(**A**) I know you can   (**C**) They say it is
(**B**) I know they will (**D**) I'm sure it will

PART TWO

Each sentence has four underlined words or phrases. The four underlined parts of the sentence are marked A, B, C, and D. Circle the letter of the <u>one</u> underlined word or phrase that is NOT CORRECT.

Example

People in <u>every part</u> of the world now <u>readily</u> and easily <u>communicates</u>
        A   B   C

    A B Ⓒ D

<u>by means</u> of electronic mail.
  D

11. When the motorist was stopped by the police for speeding, he realized that

    A B C D

he <u>must</u> <u>have</u> <u>been</u> <u>paying</u> more attention to the speed limit.
   A   B   C   D

12. Detective Holmes realized that Spencer <u>must</u> not have <u>committed</u> the murder
                                   A   B

    A B C D

on July 4th because Spencer himself <u>had</u> <u>died</u> on July 3rd.
                         C   D

13. According to the meteorologists, the hurricane <u>was supposed to hit</u> southern
                                            A

    A B C D

Florida around midnight, but in fact, it <u>did</u>; the storm <u>went</u> out over the
                               B   C

ocean and <u>didn't hit</u> any land area at all.
       D

14. Bolivia is <u>a</u> landlocked country <u>with</u> a mountainous <u>topography, and</u> so <u>does</u>
       A   B   C   D

    A B C D

Switzerland.

15. Because the little boy <u>was able</u> <u>to speak</u> both English and French perfectly,   **A B C D**
                  A   B

    his kindergarten teacher concluded that his parents <u>must</u> <u>spoke</u> French at
                                            C   D

    home.

16. Many people think <u>that</u> eating starches <u>is</u> all right because they believe that   **A B C D**
                        A   B

    starches <u>do not</u> contain large amounts of fat; however, <u>it does</u>.
              C   D

17. Because of the storm, the electricity went out and people <u>must have</u> <u>use</u>   **A B C D**
                                                  A   B

    candles <u>in order</u> <u>to see</u>.
             C   D

18. You haven't <u>ever</u> met my brother, <u>haven't</u> you? You <u>should meet</u> him because   **A B C D**
                  A   B   C

    you and he <u>could talk</u> about politics and agree on everything.
               D

19. Although some desert plants <u>can</u> <u>survive</u> without much water, most plants   **A B C D**
                              A   B

    and all animals <u>should</u> <u>have</u> plenty in order to live.
                     C   D

20. Nobody knows what happened to the Mayan civilization about A.D. 800, but   **A B C D**

    some researchers <u>believe</u> that fierce, warlike enemies <u>might</u> <u>had</u> <u>driven</u> them
                     A   B   C   D

    from their homes.

Test: Units 7–10

PART ONE

Circle the letter of the correct answer to complete each sentence.

Example

Dolphins, _____ porpoises, are well known for their ability to delight humans with their antics.   **A**   **B**   Ⓒ   **D**

(**A**) alike   (**C**) like
(**B**) that they are like   (**D**) which are alike

1. Nutritionists generally agree that it is good to eat _____ fruit, but little beef.   **A**   **B**   **C**   **D**

    (**A**) a number of   (**C**) either
    (**B**) a great deal of   (**D**) many

2. On much of television today, _____ more frequently presented than straightforward information.   **A**   **B**   **C**   **D**

    (**A**) a sensational news is   (**C**) sensational news are
    (**B**) sensational news is   (**D**) some sensational news are

3. There are few, if any, _____ more important than honesty in the assessment of a person's character.   **A**   **B**   **C**   **D**

    (**A**) criterion that is   (**C**) criterias that is
    (**B**) criteria that are   (**D**) criterions that are

4. _____ certain molds and fungi to multiply very rapidly.   **A**   **B**   **C**   **D**

    (**A**) A tropical weather   (**C**) The tropical weather
          causes   cause
    (**B**) Tropical weathers cause (**D**) Tropical weather causes

5. After the flood, many schools remained closed for several days because of the concern about _____.   **A**   **B**   **C**   **D**

    (**A**) a health   (**C**) children health
    (**B**) some health   (**D**) health

6. A false stereotype that used to exist was that _____ usually tense and nervous.   **A**   **B**   **C**   **D**

    (**A**) thin people is   (**C**) thin people are
    (**B**) a thin people is   (**D**) thin peoples are

7. Augusta Ada Byron, _____, created a program for a theoretical computer in   **A B C D**
   the mid-19th century.

   (A) a visionary English   **(C)** an English woman
       woman mathematician   visionary mathematician
   (B) a visionary woman   **(D)** a visionary English
       English mathematician   mathematician woman

8. The Great Depression of 1929 caused the loss of millions of _____ almost   **A B C D**
   impossible to find.

   (A) the jobs, and the work   **(C)** jobs, and work was
       was
   (B) job, and work was   **(D)** jobs, and works were

9. Although a third party has exhibited some political strength from time to   **A B C D**
   time, the United States essentially has _____ political system.

   (A) two parties   **(C)** the two parties'
   (B) a two parties   **(D)** a two-party

10. Not _____ from South Africa, although most of the world's supply does   **A B C D**
    originate there.

    (A) every gold comes   **(C)** all gold comes
    (B) all gold come   **(D)** every gold come

PART TWO

Each sentence has four underlined words or phrases. The four underlined parts of the sentence are marked A, B, C, and D. Circle the letter of the <u>one</u> underlined word or phrase that is NOT CORRECT.

Example

People in <u>every part</u> of the world now <u>readily</u> and easily <u>communicates</u>   **A B Ⓒ D**
          A   B   C
<u>by means</u> of electronic mail.
  D

11. People used to go to <u>horses</u> races in ancient Egypt, but the organized <u>sport</u>   **A B C D**
                   A   B
<u>dates</u> from <u>12th-century</u> England.
  C   D

12. Well adapted to <u>long, cold winters</u>, Eskimos have traditionally obtained   **A B C D**
                    A
<u>all their food</u>, <u>clothings</u>, oil, tools, and weapons from <u>sea mammals</u>.
  B   C   D

13. <u>Hypnosis</u>, the term for <u>a psychological state</u> which superficially resembles   **A B C D**
    A   B
<u>a sleep</u>, is generally induced by the monotonous repetition <u>of words</u> and
  C   D
gestures while the subject is completely relaxed.

14. <u>Much of</u> a person's character, psychologists believe, is formed by the
    A

    environmental <u>influences</u> of <u>the five first</u> years <u>of life</u>.
              B   C   D

    A B C D

15. <u>A current medical</u> advice from <u>authorities</u> warns travelers not to visit
    A   B

    <u>those areas</u> where there are epidemics of <u>cholera and malaria</u>.
    C   D

    A B C D

16. On a clear night on <u>the western plains</u>, far from <u>the lights</u> of <u>the city</u>, <u>moon</u>
                       A   B   C   D

    and stars shine brightly and appear very close.

    A B C D

17. In the 1920s and 1930s, <u>new furniture style</u> called Art Deco, which featured
                           A

    <u>more</u> comfortable, informal <u>furniture</u> with <u>little decoration</u>, became
    B   C   D

    internationally fashionable.

    A B C D

18. <u>Baseball</u> is <u>a popular sport</u> not only in <u>the United States</u>, but in Venezuela,
    A   B   C

    Dominican Republic, Mexico, and other countries as well.
    D

    A B C D

19. The largest country in area in <u>the Western Hemisphere</u>, Brazil is <u>only country</u>
                                 A   B

    in <u>the hemisphere</u> where <u>Portuguese</u> is the official language.
       C   D

    A B C D

20. Technically, <u>tomato</u> is <u>a fruit</u>, although it is commonly considered <u>a vegetable</u>
                 A   B   C

    because of its uses in <u>salads and sauces</u>.
                           D

    A B C D

Test: Units 11–12

PART ONE

Circle the letter of the correct answer to complete each sentence.

Example

Dolphins, _____ porpoises, are well known for their ability to delight humans with their antics.

A B Ⓒ D

(**A**) alike
(**B**) that they arc like

(**C**) like
(**D**) which are alike

1. Tulips, _____ into Holland in 1554, were quickly and highly valued, and by the 1630s they became the objects of wild financial speculation in Europe.

A B C D

(**A**) which introduced
(**B**) that they were introduced

(**C**) which introduced them
(**D**) introduced

2. Concepts of modern nursing were founded by Florence Nightingale, an English nurse _____ was to take care of the sick and the war-wounded.

A B C D

(**A**) that her purpose in life
(**B**) of whom her purpose in life

(**C**) whose purpose in life
(**D**) that whose purpose in life

3. Relics _____ accidentally while constructing a new subway line in Mexico City yielded new information about previous civilizations in the area.

A B C D

(**A**) that workers found them
(**B**) which workers they found

(**C**) that they were found by workers
(**D**) that workers found

4. The advanced course in astrophysics will be open only to those graduate students _____ a grade point average of 3.8 or above.

A B C D

(**A**) having
(**B**) they will have

(**C**) have
(**D**) whom have

5. Marcella served a wonderful seafood stew _____ several kinds of fish and mysterious spices.

A B C D

(**A**) which consisting of
(**B**) consisted of

(**C**) consisting of
(**D**) which it consisted of

6. Ships traveling in the North Atlantic during the winter must be constantly vigilant to avoid icebergs, large masses of ice _____ only one-ninth is visible above water.   **A B C D**

(**A**) which
(**B**) of which
(**C**) that
(**D**) of that

7. The Olympic Games, _____ in 776 B.C., did not include women participants until 1912.   **A B C D**

(**A**) they were first played
(**B**) first played
(**C**) that they were first played
(**D**) which they were first played

8. One of the great fiction writers in English, Charles Dickens portrayed all aspects of societal abuses, _____ child labor, debt imprisonment, and legal injustices.   **A B C D**

(**A**) which are including
(**B**) that they include
(**C**) included
(**D**) including

9. *The Mikado*, a warm-hearted comedy of a country _____, is one of the best-loved works of the English operetta composers Gilbert and Sullivan.   **A B C D**

(**A**) which they knew nothing about
(**B**) that they knew nothing about it
(**C**) about that they knew nothing
(**D**) they know nothing about it

10. Few visitors to Walt Disney World in Florida are aware that much of its electrical power comes from the energy _____ by burning its own garbage.   **A B C D**

(**A**) that produces
(**B**) producing
(**C**) which it is produced
(**D**) it produces

PART TWO

Each sentence has four underlined words or phrases. The four underlined parts of the sentence are marked A, B, C, and D. Circle the letter of the <u>one</u> underlined word or phrase that is NOT CORRECT.

Example

People in <u>every part</u> of the world now <u>readily</u> and easily <u>communicates</u>   **A B Ⓒ D**
       A   B   C
<u>by means</u> of electronic mail.
  D

11. South of San Francisco lies a region now <u>known as</u> Silicon Valley, <u>which</u>   **A B C D**
                                       A   B

name alludes to the silicon <u>used</u> in the many high-technology industries
                            C

<u>located</u> there.
  D

12. Sunlight sometimes filters through rain droplets in a way <u>that forms</u>   **A B C D**
     A

a rainbow, which <u>it is</u> an arc <u>composed</u> of every color in the spectrum,
         B   **C**

and is <u>regarded</u> in many places of the world as a sign of good luck.
       D

13. Japanese, <u>which spoken</u> by more than 100 million people, <u>most of whom live</u>   **A B C D**
              A   **B**

in Japan, appears to be different from <u>any other</u> language <u>spoken</u> in Asia.
                                       C   **D**

14. *Genius* is a term <u>which</u> may be used to describe a person <u>who</u> <u>he has</u> a high   **A B C D**
                    A   **B** **C**

intelligence or a special aptitude <u>in a certain field</u>.
                                   D

15. In a medical study of nearly 5,000 adults, <u>half of them</u> were given one aspirin   **A B C D**
                                                A

a day and the other half <u>given</u> a placebo, it was found that those <u>taking</u>
                          B   **C**

aspirin suffered 38 percent fewer heart attacks than those <u>who weren't</u>.
                                                           D

16. A fact <u>not widely known</u> is <u>that</u> Theodore Roosevelt, <u>that</u> vigorously   **A B C D**
            A   **B**   **C**

took part in many outdoor activities, had been a weak and sickly child

<u>who suffered</u> from asthma.
D

17. In recent decades, educated women have been marrying later, <u>that</u> means   **A B C D**
                                                               A

<u>that they</u> have fewer years <u>in</u> <u>which</u> to produce offspring.
B   **C** **D**

18. "Industrial revolution" is a term <u>which</u> <u>applies</u> to the social and economic   **A B C D**
                                     A   **B**

changes <u>that</u> <u>they mark</u> the transition of a society from an agricultural one to
        C   **D**

an industrial one.

19. Spaghetti, widely <u>believed</u> to be a dish <u>originating</u> in Italy, was actually   **A B C D**
                       A   **B**

brought there from China, <u>to where</u> Marco Polo had <u>traveled</u> at the
                          C   **D**

end of the 13th century.

20. Many older couples, at a time <u>when they</u> are still healthy and active, move to   **A B C D**
                                  A

a retirement community in order to meet people <u>with whom</u> to socialize, and
                                               B

to participate in activities <u>they</u> <u>enjoy them</u>.
                             C   **D**

Answer Key for Tests

Correct responses for Part Two questions appear in parentheses.

UNITS 1–3

Part One

1.	C	6.	A
2.	C	7.	B
3.	B	8.	B
4.	A	9.	D
5.	D	10.	D

Part Two

11. A (have been eroding)
12. B (inscribed)
13. A (believe)
14. D (would)
15. C (tastes)
16. B (were sleeping)
17. B (clear)
18. A (have quadrupled)
19. C (will have been traveling)
20. C (sounds)

UNITS 4–6

Part One

1.	B	6.	A
2.	C	7.	B
3.	B	8.	D
4.	C	9.	A
5.	D	10.	B

Part Two

11. A (should)
12. A (could)
13. B (didn't)
14. D (is)
15. D (speak)
16. D (they do)
17. A (had to)
18. B (have)
19. C (must)
20. C (have)

UNITS 7–10

Part One

1.	B	6.	C
2.	B	7.	A
3.	B	8.	C
4.	D	9.	D
5.	D	10.	C

Part Two

11. A (horse)
12. C (clothing)
13. C (sleep)
14. C (the first five)
15. A (Current medical)
16. D (the moon)
17. A (a new furniture style)
18. D (the Dominican Republic)
19. B (the only country)
20. A (the tomato / a tomato)

UNITS 11–12

Part One

1.	D	6.	B
2.	C	7.	B
3.	D	8.	D
4.	A	9.	A
5.	C	10.	D

Part Two

11. B (whose)
12. B (is)
13. A (which is spoken / spoken)
14. C (has)
15. A (half of whom)
16. C (who)
17. A (which)
18. D (mark)
19. C (where)
20. D (enjoy)

Notes

Notes

Notes